THE BOY SEX OFFENDER
AND
HIS LATER CAREER

PATTERSON SMITH REPRINT SERIES IN
CRIMINOLOGY, LAW ENFORCEMENT, AND SOCIAL PROBLEMS

A listing of publications in the SERIES *will be found at rear of volume*

PUBLICATION NO. 59: PATTERSON SMITH REPRINT SERIES IN
CRIMINOLOGY, LAW ENFORCEMENT, AND SOCIAL PROBLEMS

THE BOY SEX OFFENDER

AND

HIS LATER CAREER

By

LEWIS J. DOSHAY, M.D., Ph.D.

*Psychiatrist, Children's Courts, New York City; formerly Senior
Assistant Physician, Manhattan State Hospital, New York, and
Attending Specialist in Neuropsychiatry, U. S. Veterans Hospital,
New York City.*

Foreword by

GEORGE W. HENRY, M.D.

*Associate Professor of Clinical Psychiatry, Cornell University Medical
College; Consulting Psychiatrist, Department of Correction, New York
City; Attending Psychiatrist, New York Hospital.*

Montclair, New Jersey

PATTERSON SMITH

1969

SBN 87585-059-6

Library of Congress Catalog Card Number: 69-14921

FOREWORD

In spite of the many opportunities for enlightenment regarding sex problems, we must admit that we continue to be generally uninformed and without much prospect of improvement. If we are personally involved, we become panicky lest the facts be disclosed; if someone else is involved, particularly a socially prominent person, we are eager to learn all of the scandalous details. This unwholesome attitude toward sex is so deeply rooted in humans that it is rare to find a person who remains objective.

Social taboos are too rigid to permit adjustment to individual needs. We should continue to aspire to high standards of conduct, but failures should be evaluated in terms of each individual's ability to meet these standards. Instead, we are apt to become emotionally involved, and our resistance to frank consideration of sexual matters may contribute to the very distortions in sexual expression that we condemn.

Even in medical circles the so-called scientific topics are regularly given preference. A physician who chooses to study some phase of abnormal sexual expression must assume the risk of scrutiny by his colleagues and reluctance on the part of patients to be identified with such a physician, lest they too be considered cases of sexual maladjustment.

It is reasonable to suppose that a student should have training in medical school that will fit him to deal with the sexual problems that his patients will present to him. Although sex hygiene must be of vital interest to all persons, instruction in this topic in medical schools is as yet incidental and grossly inadequate.

A few years ago a professor in a well-known medical school ventured the opinion that instruction in matters of sex should be reserved for students in their fourth year. If it were permissible to be facetious, someone might suggest that the students give a few lectures on the subject to the faculty.

Much more serious consideration is needed when the problems include abnormal sex expression or what we often call perversion. Social condemnation then reaches all concerned. We are so blinded by our own reactions to the words used in classifying "perverts" that we almost never learn much about the accused person or the circumstances that led to the offensive behavior.

With much labor, Dr. Doshay has rendered us a distinct service in acquainting us with the boy sex offender as he has come to know him in the Children's Court clinics of New York City. In this work he gives us the pertinent factors in the development of a juvenile sex offender, and as far as is possible he tells us about the subsequent career of the offender.

Dr. Doshay's work is based largely upon the observation of clinical facts rather than upon theory, and his valuable suggestions as to treatment and prevention are the result of mature reflection upon extensive clinical experience. The reports of success in court- and clinic-treated cases are beyond expectation, and these cases merit further study both as to details of psychosexual adjustment and for a longer period in adult life.

GEORGE W. HENRY

New York City
April 1943

PREFACE

In the process of examining and treating thousands of boys in the Children's Court clinics of New York City, over a period of ten years, the author was impressed by the observation that male sex delinquents very seldom return to the court or clinic because of another sex offense. The finding became more intriguing when a search of the literature failed to disclose any reference to this phenomenon, its causes, or its significance. The literature furthermore was found woefully barren of data on the entire subject of the later life course of male juvenile sex offenders, and no source book was available for sound information on the prevention, outlook, and treatment of such cases. This work was undertaken to meet these evident needs.

Healy,[1] "father" of child guidance in this country, stated in one of his numerous works, that his 19 boy sex offenders constituted too small a group on which to base conclusions concerning the subject. No other worker in the field is recorded as having contributed materially toward an understanding of the boy sex offender in relation to his later life behavior, although philosophic and theoretic dissertations, on one or another phase of boy sex problems, based on isolated cases, are available in the literature. An important field of social concern has seemingly been neglected. In line with this are the pointed remarks of an outstanding exponent of child guidance work: "I don't understand sex delinquency. Nobody understands sex delinquencies. Some day we may . . ."[2], and also the more recent remarks of a noted sex authority: "In our present state of ignorance with regard to sexual matters . . . ."[3] Evidently psychoanalysis has not fully supplied the answer on the subject of sex, as many have been led to believe.

[1] Healy, W., et al., Reconstructing Behavior in Youth, p. 41.

[2] Plant, J. S., "Understanding Sex Delinquency," in Year Book, National Probation Association, p. 203.

[3] Henry, G. W., Sex Variants, vol. 2, p. 1025.

This investigation sheds new light on certain phases of juvenile sex delinquency. The study is limited in some aspects, but the intensive comparison of traits among two juvenile sex offender groups in relation to the adult outcomes, the rather large sampling of sexual cases employed, and the illuminating full-life case history reports, permit answers to many problems hitherto unsolved. Parts I and II afford understanding of the bearing of factors in the background on differences in personality and behavior of members of the two compared groups, as summarized in Table 20 (p. 156). Data in chapter VIII reveal that, with the exception of 12 instances of incest with sisters, so-called good boys commit just as many and violent sexual offenses as the confirmed delinquents, indicating that forecast and treatment ought not rest on the sex offense alone. The outcomes discussed in Part III provide rich material and new thought on the course of juvenile sexual and general offenses in later years of life. Summing up, in the last part of the study, chapter XIII presents the conclusions derived from the study, and chapter XIV provides important general conclusions, as well as criteria for forecast and practical measures for prevention and treatment of juvenile sex delinquency.

The study does not claim finality; such conclusions as may be reached are to be regarded as tentative hypotheses that may be helpful to further research. It is, therefore, to be considered as a pioneering or exploratory effort. As an extensive investigation of this nature, devoted exclusively to juvenile male sex offenders and their later careers, with a thorough digest of the individual case history of each offender, and compared group trait and outcome analyses as between true sex offenders and general-delinquent sex offenders, has never been made, it is hoped that the values derived from the study will prove fruitful to workers in the field.

Intelligent parents distressed by sex problems among their offspring, probation officers confronted with the formulation of constructive plans for sex delinquents among their male charges, welfare workers wrestling with day-to-day sex incidents among cases entrusted to their care, judges upon whom rests the solemn responsibility of arriving at dispositions best suited to the reclamation of the individual sex offender, institutional authorities, educators, religious leaders, psychiatrists, research workers, and students of human behavior, should obtain helpful aids from this volume.

To the writer's knowledge, no other work exists to which one may turn for answers to such practical questions as: What is the relative significance of the various types of sex offenses? What favorable and unfavorable factors determine the later course for good or evil? What percentage of court-treated juvenile sex offenders commit sexual crimes in adult life; what percentage commit general crimes? To what extent do court- and clinic-treated cases constitute a hazard to the morals of siblings and other children? Is it safe to return boy sex offenders to their homes? What types require segregation? What types tend to cure themselves of the sex maladjustment, and under what conditions? What types and what proportion of juvenile sex offenders become homosexuals in later life? What are the best procedures of treatment for the various types of sex offenders? Is psychoanalytic treatment required in juvenile sex cases? What practical measures may be utilized to prevent sex offenses among boys? Are court- and clinic-treated cases the source of the vicious sex criminals that afflict society from time to time? How do Negro and white boys compare with regard to frequency and severity of sex offenses in juvenile and later life? To what extent does puberty affect the juvenile sex offenses and the later life outcomes? These and other vital problems are arrayed for solution in this study.

The author is deeply indebted to Professor C. E. Benson of New York University for his advice in the early planning of the work and the encouragement rendered by his wise outlook.

Acknowledgments of thanks are due to Professor P. V. West for his reading of the manuscript and his expert statistical advice and assistance; to Professors F. M. Thrasher and E. R. Wood for valuable suggestions in the organization of material; to Dr. H. W. Montague, director of the New York City Children's Court clinics, for permission to employ the clinic cases for the study; to Mr. Adolphus Ragan, administrator of the Children's Court, for permission to utilize the court records and files; to the students of the College of the City of New York, and Mr. Simon Tropp, who assisted in the preliminary assembling of material; and to the many public and private agencies, courts, institutions, etc., for invaluable and wholehearted cooperation in the gathering and submitting of data essential to the investigation.

LEWIS J. DOSHAY

New York City
April 1943

CONTENTS

Chapter I

INTRODUCTION

PURPOSE OF THE STUDY

THE STUDY seeks to establish the significance of early sex offenses among males in relation to later life behavior. It is based upon comparative group analyses of early traits and adult outcomes in two essential types, comprising 256 juvenile sexual cases that had been studied and treated at the New York City Children's Court clinics between June, 1928, and June, 1934. At the time of the clinic study, the boys were within the age range of 7 to 16 years, but at present they are anywhere from 16 to 28 years of age, thus presenting a fair cross section of the stage of life when criminal tendencies fully manifest themselves.[1]

SCOPE OF THE PROBLEM

The use of the six-year period since a child's last treatment at the clinic, as an adequate minimal interval to represent later life behavior, is warranted by researches in allied fields.[2] From the minimum, however, the interval widens to twelve years, permitting a more substantial measure of adult life. This also serves to provide a larger sampling of sex cases, so that conclusions for prediction and treatment may be available, con-

[1] The *Seventh Annual Report* of the Commissioner of Correction, State of New York, 1936 (p. 220), shows that close to half of the reported 24,099 male adult law violators were within the range from 16 to 26 years of age. Goring, C. B., states: "The average age of criminals at their first conviction is about 22 years. . . . The commonest age for recruiting of criminals is between 15 and 20": *The English Convict*, pp. 123–24.

[2] Many authors employ a period of two to five years from the time of the original study and treatment as a gauge of later behavior. Thus, Healy, W., and Bronner, F. A., in *New Light on Juvenile Delinquency*, chap. xii, make use of a two- to three-year interval, while Glueck, S., and Glueck, E. T., in *One Thousand Juvenile Delinquents* (p. 6), employ a five-year period.

1

sidering that boy sex offenders constitute a small proportion of the total number of delinquents that appear in the juvenile courts and clinics.

The sex offenses among the cases studied include a variety of violations of the social codes, such as lewdness, voyeurism, excessive masturbation, exhibitionism, fornication, assault, incest, and passive or active perverted practices with juveniles or adults of the same sex (see Table 11, p. 72).

The cases studied in the clinics reached the children's courts through private and public institutions, social welfare agencies, parents, and guardians, as well as officers of the law. They therefore represent a fair cross section of boys' sex offenses in the community.

Sex offenses among girls[3] involve a totally different set of motivations and dynamics, and the writer, having worked almost exclusively with boys at the clinics, is most intimate with their problems and personalities; hence, there is justification for limiting the study to sex offenses among boys.[4]

To render it possible to judge the juvenile sexual offenses in specific relationship to later life sexual offenses, it appeared necessary that a so-called "primary" group, having no known

---

[3] Various surveys of courts and institutions reveal that sex offenses among juvenile females occur twenty to thirty times as often, in relation to other offenses, as among juvenile males, and that, with few exceptions, the drive toward sex offenses among girls is of a totally different type: see *Juvenile Delinquents in Public Institutions*, U. S. Department of Commerce, Bureau of the Census (1933), p. 16. Substantiation of these differences is also noted in the data and comments of Healy and Bronner: "The most common offense among the females, as one might expect, is sex delinquency. . . . Of the entire group of females, 191, or almost 75 per cent, had during juvenile court age engaged in sex irregularities. . . . Comparable to the 'professionals' among the males (16 burglars, 5 holdup men, 14 thieves, 2 swindlers, 2 sex perverts), there were among the females 22 prostitutes, one thief, one swindler": *Delinquents and Criminals*, pp. 35, 36.

[4] Alexander, F., and Staub, H., justify limiting their study to male criminals thus: "The investigation is limited to males because they continue to play a dominant role, not only in criminality but in the structure of society": *The Criminal, the Judge, and the Public*, p. 33.

involvement in any offensive behavior other than sexual, should be segregated from the total of 256 cases. This group, which represents true sex offenders, is comprised of 108 cases. The remaining 148 juvenile sex offenders, who are definitely known to have engaged in a mixed set of offenses, such as stealing, burglary, desertion of home, ungovernableness, or truancy, in addition to the sexual offenses, will be distinguished hereafter as the "mixed" group, representing boys of the general-delinquent type. The mixed group will be utilized as a control group, for comparison with the primary group, in determinations of factors in the background, personality, and behavior of juveniles that stand, in relation to success or failure in later years, as criteria for prediction and treatment. Since the study is primarily concerned with the significance of early sex offenses in relation to adult behavior, all references to factors in this text will therefore carry this meaning, and not the connotation of factors causing juvenile sexual delinquency. The latter will appear only in the special section on causes of sex delinquency (chap. viii).

It is recognized that some primary group cases may have been implicated in offenses other than sexual that were undetected, or if known to the family and public, were unrevealed to the children's court. Such cases would nevertheless conform to the classification of the primary group.

MINOR RELATED PROBLEMS

Through intensive analyses of factors in home, parentage, neighborhood, and personality of the compared juvenile sex delinquents, in relation to the later life outcomes, it may be possible to establish whether a boy representative of the primary group is possessed of a different configuration for prediction and treatment as contrasted with that of a boy representative of the mixed group.

Effort will be made to establish to what extent, if any, juvenile male sex cases of either group become a menace to society during adult life, through the commission of violent sex offenses.

The investigation will seek to derive further understanding of differences in the early development, character, behavior, and outcomes of the sex delinquents, through full-life case history reports of 30 representative members of the two compared groups.

The study will seek to shed light on still other questions, such as:

1. Is there any relationship between the unfavorable factors in the early life of the male juvenile sex delinquent and his later failure to adjust to the social codes?

2. Is there any relationship between the early favorable factors in a sex case and the later successful adjustment to social requirements?

3. Are there noteworthy differences in the percentage of failure during later life among the two sex groups under consideration, and the findings of Healy and Bronner[5] and the Gluecks[6] among boys of general delinquent habits?

4. Do boys committing sex offenses after puberty fare differently in later years from those committing such offenses before puberty?

5. Since no two children are exactly alike and since some variation exists in all of us, do the outcomes and personality studies warrant the conclusion that a distinct trait deviant underlies all sex offenses, or special types of sex offenses, determining the specific conduct during early and later life? If such a uniform trait operates in these cases, is it possibly related to congenital, biologic, physical, or intellectual factors? Is it susceptible to treatment?

6. Do the outcomes of later life sustain the belief that early sex offenses permanently mar the personality of the individual and condition him to later general criminal behavior?

[5] *Op. cit.*, p. 201.
[6] *Op. cit.*, pp. 155, 197.

7. What types of male juvenile sex offenders, if any, warrant segregation; serious concern; psychiatric treatment; psychoanalytic treatment; close follow-up; change of neighborhood; shift to a different home setup; special recreational and athletic programs; school adjustments; minimum of attention?

8. Do the findings derived from the study warrant the transfer of jurisdiction and treatment of any type of male sex cases from the children's courts to the community agencies?

9. Did the justices of the juvenile courts cooperate with the clinics in the completion of programs intended for the rehabilitation of the sex delinquents?

SIGNIFICANCE OF THE STUDY

The 256 sex offenders represent all the boys' sex cases (exclusive of the feebleminded) that appeared in the juvenile court clinics of all the boroughs of New York City during a period of six years. Furthermore, lest the investigator's series appear small, it may be of interest to note, by comparison, that Healy and Bronner,[7] in a survey of 4,000 court- and clinic-treated juvenile delinquents, list only 55 boy sex offenders among them, as the largest sampling to date in the literature, and the Gluecks[8] only 9 such cases among 1,000 boys.

It should, however, be understood that the 256 cases in the study do not represent all instances of boys' sex offenses in New York City during a period of six years. Such cases are quite common occurrences in the community, but many of the offenders escape detection, or, if apprehended in the act, fail to appear in court. Nonappearance is due to a variety of reasons: shame of a family at airing a matter of sex in public; fear of parents that a court record may operate permanently against the interests of their boy; low moral standards of certain families, causing them to pay little or no heed to sex offenses among their offspring; ultraprogressive attitudes of families that

[7] *Op. cit.*, p. 127.
[8] *Op. cit.*, p. 100,

regard exhibitionism, peeping, and the like, as juvenile events along the course of normal sex evolution; prejudice of some families against all courts; wise or unwise disciplinary measures considered and employed by parents as adequate substitutes for court redirection; and the fact that some cases are carried by social agencies only. For these and other reasons, thousands upon thousands of known sex offenders are privately dealt with, sometimes impulsively, at times judiciously, and at other times perhaps injuriously. The values to be derived from the study should, therefore, be considered as not limited by the comparatively small number of sex offenders carried in juvenile courts, but rather in the light of the help they may afford unknown numbers of parents and social workers throughout the country, in their day-to-day struggles with boy sex problems in the community.

PREVIOUS RESEARCH ON THE SUBJECT

Healy presented in his *Individual Delinquent*[9] a study on the origin of offenses among children and adolescents, including a genetic theory of juvenile sex delinquency, based upon freudian psychoanalytic concepts. The case histories of several boy sex offenders appear scattered in the text, too few to be of significance for the problem. The same author later produced another study[10] bearing on the personality conflicts in a group of 40 cases, among which were a few instances of male juvenile sex delinquency. Still later, Healy, together with Bronner,[11] produced a statistical digest of 4,000 cases of juvenile delinquency, already referred to, with no treatment or organization of the male sex material to permit of any conclusions.

In another survey of outcomes among 501 general delinquents placed in foster homes, Healy notes that "the nineteen boy offenders comprise for the most part cases of masturbatory

[9] P. 353.
[10] *Mental Conflicts and Misconduct*, p. 29.
[11] *Delinquents and Criminals*, p. 127.

practices with other boys, and a few who engaged in homosexual relations with other males. The numbers are too small and the offenses too scattered to permit of drawing conclusions."[12] Healy and Alexander[13] recently produced an intensive analysis of the origin of crime, in which several male sex cases are featured. Still more recently Healy and Bronner made a comparative study[14] of the personalities of 143 juvenile delinquents and their nonoffender siblings. Here again isolated instances of sex offenses are presented, insufficient to be of significance in relation to the subject.

A notable contribution[15] to child guidance work was provided by the Gluecks, involving a survey of outcomes in a thousand boys engaged in all types of law violation. Their investigation, however, does not delve into the subject of juvenile sex delinquency, and only 9 boys are listed for sex offenses in the tables.

Kirkendall[16] describes, from the viewpoint of the club counsellor, a group of youths in their hit-and-miss efforts to adjust various sex difficulties to the level of social acceptance. Kahn[17] gives a rather subjective presentation of adult homosexual cases, which therefore is aside from the present subject. Henry[18] provides a most illuminating advance toward the understanding of male and female adult homosexuals, in his two volumes on sexual variants; however, the emphasis is on adult rather than juvenile sex abnormalities.

Krinsky and Michaels,[19] in a two-page report on adult sex problems, state that among 804 individuals referred to the Boston Psychopathic Hospital from the courts during 1934 to 1937, there were 100 sex cases, and among these 90 male

[12] *Reconstructing Behavior in Youth*, p. 41.
[13] Healy, W., and Alexander, F., *Roots of Crime*, p. 163.
[14] *New Light on Juvenile Delinquency*, pp. 160, 175.
[15] *Op. cit.*, pp. 100, 155.
[16] Kirkendall, L. A., *Sex Adjustments of Young Men*.
[17] Kahn, S., *Mentality and Homosexuality*.
[18] *Op. cit.*
[19] Krinsky, C. M., and Michaels, J. J., "A Survey of One Hundred Sex Offenders," *J. Crim. Psychopathol.*, *2*: 198, 1940.

and 10 female cases. Though there were some boys among these, the number and ages are not stated, the only qualifying remark offered by the authors being, "The ages of the men ranged from 12 years to 77." One finds similar cursory reports and works filling the shelf on the subject of sex.

Durea lists,[20] among 368 delinquent boys, 9 instances of sex violations. Lee reports on a survey[21] of outcomes in 196 cases of conduct disorders that had originally received treatment by the Bureau of Child Guidance, but there were too few boys' sex cases among them to permit derivation of values and conclusions. Slawson,[22] Moll,[23] Burt,[24] and the Thomases[25] make their contributions toward an understanding of the conflicts that underlie sex misconduct among juvenile males. Freud[26] and his school (including Pfister,[27] Kempf,[28] and others), Adler[29] and his school, and many others, expound their varied viewpoints and theories on male sexual abnormalities, based on isolated cases, but they contribute little toward the understanding of essential traits in the juvenile sex delinquent that operate for success or failure in later years, and toward criteria for prevention, prediction, and proper treatment in such cases.

PROCEDURES IN COLLECTION AND ORGANIZATION OF DATA

The methods employed in the gathering and organizing of material for the study may be briefly reviewed.

As understood, only male sex cases were utilized in this investigation. Feebleminded boys, or those showing an intelligence quotient below an arbitrary 70 on the Stanford-Binet scale, were excluded, because it was not considered desirable to

[20] Durea, M. A., *Survey of Offenses Committed by Juvenile Delinquents*, p. 62.
[21] Lee, P. R., *An Experiment in the Evaluation of Social Case Work*, p. 166.
[22] Slawson, J., *The Delinquent Boy*.
[23] Moll, A., *The Sexual Life of the Child*.
[24] Burt, C., *The Young Delinquent*.
[25] Thomas, W. I., and Thomas, D. S., *The Child in America*.
[26] Freud, S., *Collected Papers*.
[27] Pfister, A., *The Psychoanalytic Method*.
[28] Kempf, E. J., *Psychopathology*.
[29] Adler, A., *Understanding Human Nature*.

inject the factor of feeblemindedness into the study,[30] although, in general, feebleminded individuals have not been proved to respond less favorably to treatment than normals. With these exceptions, all instances of male sex delinquency found in the files of the clinics of the children's courts of the various boroughs of New York City, between June, 1928, and June, 1934, were accepted for the research, in direct sequence, precluding any possibility of selection on the basis of special advantages in the outcomes. The procedure, netting 256 cases for the study, involved a most painstaking review of many thousands of records, since sexual offenses account for less than 5 per cent of the male delinquents. Negro children were included in the series, and special comparisons of traits and outcomes will be made as between these and the white boys. There were 26 Negro and 230 white children in the series.

A detailed digest of the case record of each of the 256 boys was entered on a coded card form, especially constructed for the purpose (see Appendix, Form 1). The items, covering all the salient data with regard to parents, home, siblings, neighborhood, school, church, play, health, intelligence, temperament, and the sexual and general offenses, were transferred from the coded cards to separate summary sheets for the primary and the mixed groups respectively. The sheets supplied the material for the construction of the various frequency tables and diagrams, which permitted comparison and evaluation of each trait in the two sex groups. A review and interpretation of the various sets of traits appear in the chapter summaries. The salient traits and the pronounced differences in the two groups are set forth in a summary table in the part of the study devoted to conclusions, as factors in relation to success or failure in later life.

The following procedures were employed in tracing the later life behavior of the 256 cases: (a) the records of the probation

---

[30] Sutherland, E. H., in *Principles of Criminology* (p. 95), reveals a well-balanced study of the relationship of feeblemindedness to juvenile offenses and crime, and finds that, as a general factor, it is relatively insignificant.

department of the children's courts of the various boroughs of New York City were searched for evidence of later juvenile offenses among the cases accepted for study; (b) the services of the Social Service Exchange Clearance Bureau of New York City were utilized to gather information on adult court, prison, or institutional records among the cases studied; (c) the bureaus of criminal identification of New York City and New York State were contacted for adult criminal records among the cases; (d) adult criminal courts and correctional and penal institutions were reached to obtain specific data on violations; (e) the Juvenile Aid Bureau of the Police Department, schools, hospitals, relief agencies, and child and family welfare agencies were contacted for information on the later life behavior of these juvenile sex offenders; (f) homes were visited, and families, neighbors, and the subjects themselves were interviewed, where possible and desirable.[31]   Information gathered by these procedures was entered on the follow-up forms, which were specially constructed for this research (see Appendix, Form 2).

On the basis of the follow-up data, the cases were classified as failures in the outcomes, when there was proved evidence of a return to sexual offenses in adult life—i.e., at the age of 16 years or over, when an individual is considered past the juvenile stage, and is subject to adjudication for his unlawful acts in an adult court.

In addition, however, to the chief objective of establishing the extent to which early sex offenders return to sexually undesirable behavior in later years, the study is also concerned with evaluating the significance of early sex offenses in relation to later general criminality (p. 4).   To meet this aim, subjects committing general crimes are also counted as failures, but receive separate treatment in the analyses, interpretations, and conclusions.

---

[31] In some instances, agencies working with one or another member of the family requested that no personal contact be made and such requests were respected.   In other instances, where interviews might have prejudiced the marital or vocational status of the subject, data were gathered through other sources.

It is necessary to explain that some attention will be devoted to information obtained from various welfare agencies and home contacts, but in order to prevent bias, suspicion, heresay, and casual opinion from entering into and perverting the criterion of failure or success, this was based entirely on the presence or absence of indisputable evidence of law violation. This procedure was furthermore rendered necessary by the lack of facilities in the study for a painstaking check upon all claims and reports with regard to a delinquent, for and against him. It was warranted by the fact that the outcomes in the two compared groups could thus be evaluated on the basis of recorded and verifiable data of courts and correctional and penal institutions. Healy employed a similar criterion of failure or success:

> Without much more detailed accounts than were available, indeed, without personal contacts or re-study of the individual, it would be impossible to make fine discriminations, to evaluate success and failure in terms of use or disuse of best potentialities, or in terms of happiness or economic productivity. More specifically, outcome was to be counted a success, when the individual was living in the community without detriment to it and had engaged in no criminality (whether he presented any problems in his personality or was content with his lot, it was not considered practicable to determine). Conversely, failure denoted actual delinquency—all individuals having court records and adjudged guilty as well as those committed to correctional institutions were regarded as failures.[32]

It is recognized that objection may be raised to the criterion, on the grounds that it excludes from consideration such phases of adult misbehavior—as habitual idleness, late hours, gambling, and flirtations—as did not reach police attention and a court of record. Nevertheless, on sober reflection it should be conceded that it is very difficult to base the criterion of success or failure on such vague and controversial material, or to derive scientific determinations and conclusions from it. More specifically, the subject may deny the accusations, and perhaps

---

[32] Healy and Bronner, *Delinquents and Criminals*, pp. 19, 28.

justly, as for example by attributing his alleged "idleness" to economic factors beyond his control. He might attribute his alleged "late hours" to a desire to avoid conflict with an unfriendly stepfather in the home. To the charge of "gambling" he might retort thus: "How could I gamble when I have not earned anything in months? I play cards for a few pennies occasionally to pass time." On a charge of "flirtations" he might admit that, like other boys on the street, he engages in petty flirtations with girls, but firmly deny any violations of the sex codes.

It is evident that to pass judgment on such vague and controversial items would actually require the writer to place subjective verdicts of guilt or innocence upon the individuals, in order to render it possible to utilize the data statistically. The interests of objective precision warrant the sacrifice of disputable vague minor complaints of misconduct, and justify resting the criterion of failure or success on the presence or absence of an adult criminal court record, establishing an offense, or of commitment to a correctional or penal institution.

It is recognized that others among our cases aside from the legally recorded violators may have committed sexual and general crimes in which they were not apprehended; but since the extent and nature of such offenses are unknown, it would be idle speculation to pay more than passing attention to the circumstance. Furthermore, these would not be likely to affect materially the values in the two compared groups.

Violations of the law among the cases studied, occurring at ages earlier than 16 years, are not considered as failures, but receive separate attention in the discussion of outcomes, under the topic of "juvenile recidivism."

With this introduction regarding the purpose and need of such a study, the lack of previous research in the field, and the methods employed in the collection, organization, and analysis of the data, the reader may be better prepared to appreciate the limitations involved in such a large-scale study, as well as the significance of the values and interpretations derived.

PART I

THE BACKGROUND OF THE SEX DELINQUENT

IN ORDER to gain clearer insight into the personality traits that differentiate the primary type of sex delinquent from the mixed, and their relationship to the later life outcomes, an analysis of the background influences that mold and shape the form and development of the delinquent personality deserves first consideration. It is hoped, by such breakdown of background and personality into essential elements, to discover the basic factors that stand in relation to success or failure in later years, as sound criteria for prediction and treatment in similar cases.

Influences of home and neighborhood play upon the inherent plastic equipment of the child, in a manifest as well as intangible manner, to create the delinquent as we see him later. The old speculative view of Lombroso and his school, postulating the inheritance of criminal (and hence necessarily juvenile delinquent) traits, is no longer tenable in the light of more recent objective investigations. Reckless and Smith[1] comment on these theories as follows:

Schlapp and Smith present in *The New Criminology* some cases of the glandular effects on crime. This work is the nearest approach to the Italian school of neo-Lombrosians. In fact, Schlapp and Smith identify themselves with Lombroso, but with a new emphasis on glandular relationships to crime. The treatment is almost wholly theoretical and the number of cases definitely explained is small.[1]

Shaw, in an intensive analysis of the causative factors of delinquency, finds morbid neighborhoods to be most significant. His data reveal the following:

[1] Reckless, W. C., and Smith, M., *Juvenile Delinquency*, p. 98.

13

The boy delinquency rate in Chicago was 206 to 1,000 for a district within one mile of the center of the city; 56 for the second mile; 6 for the third mile, and none for the fourth mile.[2]

One can no longer rest delinquency on theories of heredity, when such obvious causative factors are presented. The child does not bring the psychopathic personality traits of a delinquent with him from the cradle. In this regard, Kempf remarks:

The fact that psychopathic personalities are to be found among the ancestors of a psychopath has been made the flimsy ground upon which the dogmatic thinkers in psychiatry have made the assumption of "defective heredity," "hereditary taint," "constitutional inferiority," etc. This assumption upon mature consideration is nothing less than amazing and could hardly have been wilder or more unproductive.[3]

The present investigator, in a previous research entirely devoted to the question of inheritance of mental and behavior abnormalities, commented on the same subject as follows:

Yet, facts prove that individuals carrying this neuropathic trait have not only survived to our present day, but have flourished to a point where their ratio has increased alarmingly in proportion to the "fitter" untainted types. Hence we must either conclude that this [psychotic, psychopathic, or neurotic] trait could not possibly have been inherited, since as an inferior trait it survived so successfully, or that it was inherited as a superior trait, carrying success in a struggle for existence. Unless proof can be brought in support of our present unwarranted belief in mental disease heredity, only two courses lie open to us: either we disclaim that the neuropathic constitution is inherited, or announce that it is inherited as a desirable trait. We know, unfortunately, that the neuropathic trait is not desirable, but a regressive trait, hence we must concede that it is not inherited.[4]

[2] Shaw, C. R., et al., Delinquency Areas, p. 170.
[3] Op. cit., p. 80.
[4] Doshay, L. J., "Evolution Disproves Heredity in Mental Diseases," M. J. & Rec., 1930, p. 195.

With these introductory remarks indicating the import of environment, the background factors of home, parents, and neighborhood among the members of the two compared groups will be examined.

The following topics will be treated in this part of the investigation: family and home factors among the two compared sex groups (chap. ii); factors in the personalities of the parents (chap. iii); social and community factors (chap. iv).

Chapter II

FAMILY AND HOME FACTORS

STATUS OF PARENTS

A<small>N OLD</small> fallacy to the effect that sex delinquency (often carelessly referred to as "degeneracy") in children is related to overage, underage, or great disparity in ages of the parents at the time of conception, persists in some of the literature.[1]

Age Distribution. It is of interest, therefore, to examine Table 21 (Appendix) and note that among the 256 fathers of these so-called immoral children, there were only four fathers, or 1.4 per cent in the series, above the age of 50 at the time of birth of the delinquents, that only 20.4 per cent were above 40 years of age, and that only 23 per cent of the mothers were above 35 years of age at the time of conception of the delinquents. From these figures it must be apparent that since approximately 70 per cent of the parents were under 35 years of age at the time of birth of the sex delinquents, they cannot be charged with senility, decadence, or impairment of the vitality of their offspring by reason of their overage.[2] At the age of 35, parents are in the prime of life, hence the theory that senility in parents is responsible for sex delinquency among their children is thoroughly disproved. The ages of the parents were taken as of their last birthdays.

On the other hand, immaturity of parents can hardly be regarded as the cause of sexual delinquency among their off-

[1] MacDonald, A., *Juvenile Crime and Reformation*, p. 298; also Lombroso, C., *Crime, Its Causes and Remedies*, p. 170.

[2] Groves, E. R., and Ogburn, W. F., in discussing marriage figures of the national census of 1920, reveal that no more than 75 per cent of parents had married prior to 35 years of age. Hence, if 70 per cent of the parents in this study gave birth to the delinquents before the age of 35, they surely were close to the norms: Groves, E. R., and Ogburn, W. F., *American Marriage and Family Relationships*, p. 221.

spring, since Table 21 reveals that only 5 per cent of the parents were under 20, and only 20 per cent under 25 years of age, at the time of birth of the delinquents.[3]

TABLE 1.—*Disparity in Ages of Parents of Delinquents of Primary and Mixed Groups*

Difference in Ages of Parents in Years	Primary Group (108 Cases) Percentage	Mixed Group (148 Cases)* Percentage	Both Groups (256 Cases)* Percentage
0	13.9	10.8	12.2
1	17.6	15.6	16.5
2	14.9	12.2	13.3
3	13.9	11.6	12.4
4	8.3	4.8	6.4
5	10.3	5.5	7.4
6	1.8	8.8	5.9
7	4.6	6.1	5.5
8	4.6	4.1	4.3
9	5.5	2.8	3.9
10	1.8	4.1	3.2
11	1.8	4.8	3.5
12	0.0	4.1	2.3
13	0.0	2.0	1.2
14	0.0	0.7	0.4
15	0.0	0.7	0.4
16+	0.0	1.3	1.2
Totals	100.0	100.0	100.0
Mean of differences in ages of parents	3.5 years	4.9 years	4.2 years

* Difference in ages of parents in 4 cases unknown.

Age disparity of parents as a factor in sex delinquency is readily discounted by the data in Table 1, showing that for the entire series the mean (M) of the differences in the ages of the parents is only four and one-fifth years. It is common knowledge and experience that because of economic, social, and

[3] Groves and Ogburn show that 15 per cent of parents in the United States are under 20 years of age at the time of marriage: *op. cit.*, p. 22.

psychologic factors, as well as because of the more rapid physical maturation of the female, the man is usually older than the woman at the time of marriage. However, in over 54 per cent of the cases, the disparity in the ages of the parents was no greater than three years. Such small difference between the

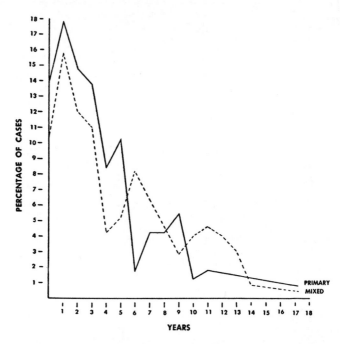

DIAGRAM 1. DISPARITY IN AGES OF PARENTS AS COMPARED FOR PRIMARY AND MIXED GROUP DELINQUENTS

ages of father and mother could not conceivably be considered a determinant of faulty inheritance in the children. It is also significant that, as the disparity in years between the parents increases, the frequency curve in Diagram 1 drops steadily, indicating that age disparity is not a cause of sex delinquency.

The disparities in this series are no greater than those found in the general population.[4]

Race. Table 22 (Appendix) and Diagram 2 reveal that 7.4 per cent of the primary group members and 12.2 per cent of the mixed group members are Negro. In the entire series there are 10.2 per cent of Negroes. This is a slightly smaller percentage of Negroes than is found among the nonsexual or

COMBINED GROUPS

| 10.2 | 89.8 |

MIXED GROUP

| 12.2 | 87.8 |

PRIMARY GROUP

| 7.4 | 92.6 |

☐ WHITE   ■ COLORED

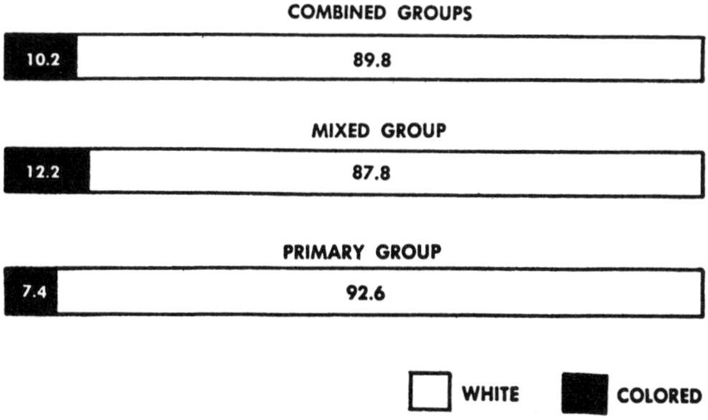

DIAGRAM 2. RACE DISTRIBUTION, SHOWN BY PERCENTAGE FIGURES, OF PARENTS AND DELINQUENTS OF PRIMARY, MIXED, AND COMBINED GROUPS

general delinquents.[5] The race of a child is always considered the same as that of its parents.

[4] An earlier age of marriage among women than among men is found in both urban and rural districts. Two factors contribute: the fact that young women mature earlier sexually, and the economic factor of support of the family. See Groves and Ogburn, *op. cit.*, p. 222.

[5] Reckless and Smith state that Negroes supply a proportion of all delinquent children greater than the proportion of Negroes in the total population. Thus in 1928, 16 per cent of all delinquent children were Negro (the Negro ratio in the total population is about 4 per cent): *op. cit.*, p. 63. Among the total of all types of delinquents appearing in the New York City children's courts in 1933, there were 17.5 per cent of Negroes: *Annual Report*, Domestic Relations Court, New York City, 1934, p. 45.

Nationality.   No outstanding differences appear between the primary and mixed group members on the score of parental nationality in Diagram 3 and Table 23 of the Appendix. About 60 per cent of the parents in each group are foreign-born, as against only 5 per cent of the delinquents themselves. While the difference between the frequency of foreign-born parents and delinquents is very pronounced, it nevertheless cannot be considered a factor in relation to the outcomes, since

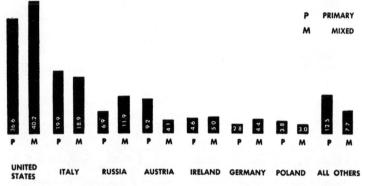

DIAGRAM 3. NATIONALITY OF PARENTS OF PRIMARY AND MIXED GROUP CASES: PERCENTAGE DISTRIBUTION

the ratios show a fairly uniform distribution in both the primary and mixed groups.

Education and Mastery of English Language Tools.   Education of parents is classified in the categories of college education, high-school education, elementary, informal, and no education. Elementary school training is noted among 75 per cent of the parents of both groups (Table 24, Appendix). There is a definite weighting of high-school education, or better, among the parents of the primary group, as compared with the mixed. Approximately 25 per cent of all the parents are unable to write or read English (Table 25, Appendix).

Income and Occupational Status.   Family income is arbitrarily classified as high, when earnings are above $15 a week per family member; as comfortable, at the level of $5 to $15 a week; and as poor, when they are below $5 a week per member. The income status of the family seems reflected as a possible factor in the lives of the children of the two compared groups, since there is a greater ratio of higher incomes in the primary group, as compared with the mixed (36 per cent in the former, 22 per cent in the latter). The poverty income class accounts for 63.6 per cent of the primary group families and 77.5 per cent of the mixed group families (Table 26, Appendix).

Higher occupational rank among fathers is found in the primary group, with four fathers listed as managers, as against none in the mixed group, and 14 per cent listed as business men, as compared with only 6 per cent in the mixed group (Table 27, Appendix).

A large portion of "unknown" income families is chargeable to broken homes, deserted, divorced, or separated parents, and fathers in mental hospitals. These families, because of the conditions instanced, very likely fall within the lower income group, though not necessarily so in specific instances.

In a recent work, Healy and Bronner[6] found that only one-third of the families of delinquents enjoyed adequate incomes, that half of the families existed on marginal incomes, and that 16 per cent were entirely dependent on public aid. They supply no comparable figures for the general population. Lund,[7] employing a control group, found that only 26.7 per cent of the nondelinquent children studied came from the economic groups that furnished 66 per cent of the delinquents.

The Gluecks comment as follows on general population statistics: "But reliable data as to the economic status of the general population are unavailable."[8]

---

[6] *New Light on Juvenile Delinquency*, p. 44.

[7] Lund, D., *Ueber die Ursachen der Jugendasozialitaet*, p. 45.

[8] Glueck, S., and Glueck, E. T., *500 Criminal Careers*, p. 113.

Shaw and McKay, however, present the following on general population data:

The coefficient of correlation between these rates of [economic] dependency and the rates of delinquents in the 1917–1923 juvenile court series is 0.74. . . . A third series of dependents used in this study included children in families which received financial aid under the provisions of the Mothers' Pension Act during 1917–1923. The rates of dependency were calculated upon the basis of the total population

TABLE 2.—*Dead and Disabled Parents in Families of Delinquents of Primary and Mixed Groups*

Groups	Physically Disabled				Mentally Disabled*				Dead				Total Dead and Disabled	
	Father		Mother		Father		Mother		Father		Mother		Both Parents	
	No.	Per-cent-age	No.	Per-cent-age	No.	Per-cent-age	No.	Per-cent-age	No.	Per-cent-age	No.	Per-cent-age	No.	Per-cent-age
Primary 108 cases	1	0.9	3	2.8	6	5.5	3	2.8	19	17.6	14	12.9	46	42.5
Mixed 148 cases	8	5.4	7	4.7	2	1.3	9	6.1	31	20.9	22	14.9	79	53.4
Primary and mixed 256 cases	9	3.5	10	3.9	8	3.1	12	4.7	50	19.5	36	14.1	125	48.7

* One case of epilepsy in one father of each group.

under 15 years of age in the 113 square mile areas. . . . When the rates for this series of dependents are correlated with the rates of delinquents in the 1917–1923 juvenile court series, the coefficient is 0.63.[9]

Dead and Disabled Parents. Parents are listed in Table 2 as disabled if they are afflicted with severe mental or physical ailments, if they are crippled in body or mind, or if they are

[9] Shaw, C. R., and McKay, H. D., *Social Factors in Juvenile Delinquency*, Report on the Causes of Crime, National Commission on Law Observance, vol. 2, pp. 76–77.

inmates of a mental or tuberculosis hospital. It must be apparent that no mild physical ailments are considered, since the figures in that case would have been many times as large.

There is a greater frequency of dead and disabled parents among mixed group delinquents than among the primary (53.4 per cent as against 42.5 per cent). Among the 256 cases of the two groups, there are 86 dead parents, or 34 per cent, and 39 seriously disabled parents, or 16 per cent.

Grimberg presents[10] the following figures on deaths among parents of delinquents: out of a total of 498 cases, mothers were dead in 107 cases, or 21 per cent, fathers dead in 93 cases, or 19 per cent, and both parents dead in 37 cases, or 8 per cent. Grimberg's figures are slightly higher than those given above, probably owing to a difference in sampling, but they nevertheless serve to indicate the high mortality incidence among parents of delinquents.

The findings in this study reveal that almost 50 per cent of the children of the two groups are affected by death or serious disability among the parents.

HOME STATUS

Housing Conditions and Crowding. Housing conditions are arbitrarily classified under the headings of owned homes, high rent ($10 or more per person per month), average rent ($5 to $10 a month per person), and low rent (less than $5 monthly per person). Rent per person is employed rather than rent per room, since it is conceivable that five persons might occupy one crowded and cheaply furnished room, and yet, because the rent may be $15 per month, the impression would be gained that these individuals are living in comfort and luxury.

In the primary group are found 18.5 per cent of owned homes, as against only 8.3 per cent of owned homes in the mixed group (see Table 28, Appendix). There is a suggestion that more than a reasonable portion of the earnings are expended on

---

[10] Grimberg, L., *Emotion and Delinquency*, p. 29.

housing among the poor families, since, although a total of 71.8 per cent of the 256 families are classified as poverty income types, only 26.7 per cent of them are found classified as living in low-rent homes.   The discrepancy may, however, be accounted for by factors such as agency supplemental assistance, differences in the levels considered as low income and low housing, and so on.   There is, nevertheless, indication that the poor families are sacrificing more than a reasonable share of their income for housing, to the probable exclusion of such vital needs as adequate food, clothing, and recreation.

Crowding refers to the condition of more than two occupants to a room, and is found among 27 per cent of the mixed group cases, and 20 per cent of the primary.   Burt found[11] crowding in the homes of delinquents 1.32 times as frequent as in the nondelinquent population, but did not believe that crowding was a factor of importance in delinquency.   Garrison notes that "overcrowding is likely to occur in circumstances of poverty and leads to stealing."[12]

Broken Homes.   A broken home is one in which there has been either death of a parent, a divorce or separation of parents, or desertion of a parent.   Even in instances where there is remarriage of a widow or widower, the home is nevertheless considered broken, since the original status with regard to the child no longer exists.

Table 3 and Diagram 4 show that in the primary group there are slightly fewer broken homes than in the mixed group —43.4 per cent as against 50 per cent.

Among the white boys, there is a slight margin of preponderance of intact homes, but among the Negroes broken homes occur more than twice as often as unbroken homes; furthermore, if the five British West Indian Negro families with unbroken homes were excluded, the ratio of broken to intact

[11] *Op. cit.*, p. 85.
[12] Garrison, K. C., *The Psychology of Adolescence*, p. 352.

TABLE 3.—*Broken and Unbroken Homes (Families of Delinquents of Primary and Mixed Groups)*

Groups	Broken Homes						Unbroken Homes						Total	
	White		Negro		Total		White		Negro		Total			
	No.	Percentage	No.	Percentage	No.	Percentage	No.	Percentage	No.	Percentage	No.	Percentage	No.	Percentage
Primary 108 cases	41	37.9	6	5.5	47	43.4	59	54.7	2	1.9	61	56.6	108	100
Mixed 148 cases	62	41.2	12	8.8	74	50.0	68	46.0	6*	4.0	74	50.0	148	100
Total primary and mixed 256 cases	103	40.3	18	7.0	121	47.3	127	49.6	8	3.1	135	52.7	256	100

* Five of the Negro families are British West Indian. If these were excluded, the total of Negro (American) unbroken homes would be 3, or 1.2 per cent of the series.

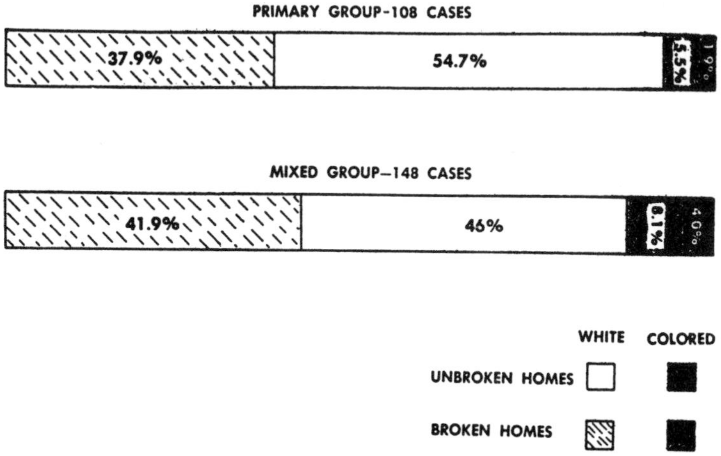

PRIMARY GROUP-108 CASES

37.9%   54.7%   1.9%

MIXED GROUP—148 CASES

41.9%   46%   0.1%   4.0%

	WHITE	COLORED
UNBROKEN HOMES	□	■
BROKEN HOMES	▨	■

DIAGRAM 4. BROKEN AND UNBROKEN HOMES AMONG FAMILIES OF PRIMARY AND MIXED GROUP DELINQUENTS

"Broken home" signifies that one or both parents are dead or have deserted, or that parents are divorced or separated.

homes among the American Negro families would be still more striking.

Shideler estimated[13] that only 25.3 per cent of children in the total population come from families broken by death, divorce, or separation. On the other hand, his study of 7,598 juvenile delinquents in industrial schools of 31 states indicates that 50.7 per cent of the subjects come from such broken homes. He therefore finds that juvenile delinquency and broken homes correlate highly.

Reckless and Smith remark as follows on the broken home: "It would seem that a loosening of the family controls cannot be expected to result in anything save an increase in delinquency. For it is in early life that foundations of habits called self-control are laid down."[14]

Shaw and McKay, in a carefully controlled study, however, report the following significant data on the subject of the broken home:

The rate of broken homes among 1,675 delinquents is, therefore, 42.5, while the rate among the 1,675 boys in the control group is 36.1. . . . The greatest difference is in the Negro group, where the actual rate of broken homes among the delinquents is 66 per cent, and the expected rate in the control group is 50.6 per cent. . . . In the American group the rate of broken homes is 40.5 in the delinquent, and 35.3 in the control group; Italian broken homes, 27 per cent in the delinquent and 24 per cent in the control group. . . . It was found that the difference between the rates in the delinquent and the control groups furnished a very inadequate basis for the conclusion that the broken home is an important factor in delinquency.[15]

Since the frequency of broken homes is almost similar in the two groups, it is not a factor that is likely to bear on the outcomes.

[13] Shideler, E. H., "Family Disintegration and the Delinquent Boy in the United States," *J. Crim. Law & Criminol.*, 8: 713, 1918.

[14] *Op. cit.*, pp. 18, 126.

[15] *Op. cit.*, pp. 275, 276, 284.

Social Aid. Social aid denotes any dependency of the family upon community agencies, such as child welfare, family welfare, physical and mental welfare, or on child guidance clinics, etc.

Data on various forms of social aid present significant differences in the two compared groups, with only 27.7 per cent of the primary group families so participating, as against 47.2 per cent of the mixed group (Table 29, Appendix). The critical ratio (CR) of the difference in the two groups is 3.4, indicating definite reliability.

Total dependency on all forms of social aid occurred in but 2.8 per cent of the primary group, as against 10.1 per cent of the mixed group families. In a carefully conducted and controlled study, Healy and Bronner found[16] that 16 per cent of the families of delinquents were entirely dependent on public aid.

The difference in the amount of social aid sought by the two groups suggests that fundamental variations very likely exist in the personality, management, and constructiveness of the parents. It is of interest to note that while the poor-income families in the mixed group total 77 per cent as against 63 per cent in the primary group, 47 per cent of the mixed group families sought social aid, as against only 27 per cent of the primary. This disparity may in part be due to the slightly greater ratio of broken homes in the mixed group, but it may also be due to a lower pride and sense of social responsibility among the mixed group families, so that they turn more readily to public assistance, as compared with members of the primary group. The frequency of "all types of social aid" among mixed group families is suggestive of considerable social, physical, and possible moral decay in the homes, which may serve as determinants of delinquent attitudes and behavior among the children, and hence may operate as factors in relation to later life behavior.

[15] *New Light on Juvenile Delinquency,* p. 44.

SIBLING STATUS

Ordinal Position.   The ordinal position of a child in a family refers to its place in the sequence of birth—i.e., as the oldest, second oldest, etc., or the youngest in the family.   Considerable attention is paid in the literature, especially by the Adlerian school of psychology,[17] to the importance of a child's ordinal position in relation to his particular type of behavior.

It is to be noted, in Table 30 of the Appendix, that in the primary group there is a greater distribution of sex cases among the youngest children than there is in the mixed group.   The difference may be due to greater docility and physical infirmity (this will receive attention in Part II) among primary group boys, leading to a greater submissiveness to immorality among the youngest of them.   Intermediate children appear in greater frequency in the mixed group, which may be accounted for by the fact that, in addition to sex offenses, these boys regularly engaged in general delinquencies, which require a more aggressive and sturdier body than is likely to be possessed by the youngest of them.   The lower frequency among the oldest children of both groups is, in part, explained by the children's court age limit of 16 years.

In the complete series of 256 cases, the youngest ordinal position obtains in 62 instances or 24.2 per cent (Table 31, Appendix), the oldest in 54 instances, or 21.2 per cent; the "only" child is found in 30 instances, or 11.7 per cent, and the intermediate position accounts for 110 cases, or 43 per cent of the series.[18]

---

[17] Adler remarks on the ordinal position: "The striving for power of a second-born child has its especial nuance. . . . These children are always under pressure. . . . The older has usurped the place of importance in the family": *op. cit.*, p. 84.

[18] On the ordinal position of 153 delinquents, Healy notes that oldest children constituted 25 per cent of the cases, youngest 12 per cent, and intermediate 63 per cent of the cases: Healy and Bronner, *op. cit.*, p. 52.   Hirsch submits the following on ordinal position of delinquents: eldest, 24 per cent; intermediate, 50.4 per cent; youngest, 17.6 per cent; only child, 8 per cent: Hirsch, N. D., *Dynamic Causes of Juvenile Crime*, p. 84.

Except that there is a slightly greater tendency for youngest children in the primary group, and intermediate children in the mixed group, to become involved in sexual offenses, the ordinal position of a child is apparently not a factor to consider for relationship to the outcomes.

Siblings. Sibling is a term applied to a brother or sister, i.e., an issue of both parents of the delinquent. The term step-sibling denotes that the so-called brother or sister stands in relation to the delinquent only accidentally through the re-marriage of one of the parents, and that the issue is from neither of the true parents of the delinquent (i.e., no blood relationship). Half-sibling denotes that the so-called brother or sister is an issue of one parent of the delinquent.

It is interesting to note the rather small ratio (11 per cent) of families, in the total series of 256 cases, with step- or half-siblings (Table 32, Appendix), when considered in the light of the high frequency of broken homes. Step- and half-siblings are uniformly distributed among the primary and mixed group sex delinquents (11.1 per cent and 10.8 per cent, respectively).

Criminal Siblings. This item covers instances of juvenile offenses as well as adult crimes and jail sentences among siblings. It is found among 12.8 per cent of the mixed group cases, as against 6.4 per cent of the primary group (Table 33)—exactly twice the frequency in the mixed group as compared with the primary. This difference approaches reliability, since the critical ratio is 1.9. Approximately 10 per cent of the entire series of 256 subjects have one or more siblings with court or prison record, only 1.2 per cent of the 256 cases have two or more siblings with criminal records, and only 0.4 per cent have three such siblings.

Criminalism among siblings implies a possible undermining of ethical standards within the home and unhealthy influences bearing upon the other siblings. The same consideration applies to criminal parents (chap. iii). Shaw and McKay comment on this as follows:

The extremely high rate of crime among the young men between 17 and 21 years of age, living in the areas with high rates of juvenile delinquency, is convincing proof of the presence of criminal influences surrounding the boys in these areas. . . . The presence of a large number of older offenders in a neighborhood is a fact of great significance for the understanding of the problem of juvenile delinquency.[19] . . . In some cases delinquent and criminal patterns of behavior are transmitted through the personal contacts within the family group.[20]

SUMMARY

Conditions in the home and family seem regularly to favor the children of the primary group, as against the mixed group, on the score of parents' education, parents' occupational status, family income, housing conditions, social dependency, dead and disabled parents, criminal siblings, etc.

Among the unfavorable factors, dependency on public aid is significantly weighted in the mixed group, with 47.2 per cent of the families scored for this point, as compared with 27.7 per cent in the primary group. This is equal to a critical ratio of 3.4, indicating that definite reliability exists in the difference. Criminal siblings are found among 12.8 per cent of the mixed group members, as compared with 6.4 per cent of the primary group, giving a critical ratio of difference of 1.9, reflecting some degree of reliability.

Other unfavorable home conditions than those considered in this chapter may have had bearing on the children under study, but, because of vagueness and immeasurability, they have not obtained statistical treatment and evaluation. Among these may be mentioned the rejection of a child by a parent, employment of a child by one parent to spy on the other, unreasonable restriction of a child's play life, burdening of a child's mind with economic, physical, and marital problems of the parents, permitting of grown children to sleep together, mismanagement of a highly sensitive, neurotic, or bed-wetting

[19] *Op. cit.*, p. 127.
[20] *Ibid.*, p. 135.

child, etc. It should be understood, moreover, that the human personality is an extremely complex mechanism, and, whereas a seemingly trivial remark or event may miss one child altogether, it may profoundly disturb the life of another. Healy and Bronner, in a comparative study of delinquent and nondelinquent siblings from apparently similar backgrounds, place[21] great emphasis on the importance of these intangible and immeasurable factors. Ira Wile states: "Many morbid influences in the home never reach us; there are more subtle influences at work in the home, and many a home atmosphere, which to the casual observer may appear beneficial, is, nevertheless, harmful."[22]

The tangible item of mental deficiency in the parents may operate as a potent factor[23] in the conduct and management of the home and children, but, since no dependable data exist in our records to permit of precise determinations of its frequency and severity, it is omitted. Although the parents report at the court clinics, and are regularly interviewed, they are not examined psychometrically as a routine, and haphazard opinions as to feeblemindedness are unreliable for statistical digest.

The finding that 50 per cent of the children of both groups are affected by death or serious disability of the parents, when considered in conjunction with other factors that have been discussed or will be treated later, serves to reflect the tremendous amount of social pathology[24] generally operating in the lives

[21] *Op. cit.*, chap. v.

[22] Wile, I. S., *The Challenge of Childhood*, p. 7.

[23] The Gluecks, in *One Thousand Delinquents* (p. 78) state that feeblemindedness among the parents of delinquents occurred in *probably* 19 per cent of cases.

[24] Healy and Bronner (*op. cit.*, p. 130) state that quarreling of a serious nature was found in 12 per cent of homes of general delinquents; alcoholism, immorality, and criminalism among 21 per cent of the parents; that nearly half the cases came from homes broken by death, desertion, divorce, or separation; and that among 2,000 young repeat offenders, reasonably good home conditions for the upbringing of a child existed in only 7.6 per cent of the cases. [This represents an alarming revelation of the extent of morbidity in the background of cases of general delinquency, which are of a type similar in behavior, except for the sex offenses, to the cases of the mixed group.]

of the children under investigation, with the disadvantages consistently weighted in the mixed group thus far. The item of broken homes, however, being almost equally distributed in the two groups, does not appear to be a factor in one group as compared with the other.

While only a few of the *favorable home and family traits*, such as high income, good housing, higher educational status, etc., show fairly reliable differences in the two groups, the evidence of a consistent trend is nevertheless important. It is realized that many factors in one case, or one factor in an entire group, could not materially alter the status or prospects of a group; but when many factors regularly tend to favor one group as against another, they bear significance. Thus, the total of the favorable home and family factors in the primary group is 72.2 per cent, as against 35.0 per cent in the mixed, with a critical ratio of the difference equal to 6.4, which denotes high reliability.

The differences in the favorable and unfavorable home conditions of the two compared groups should bear significantly on differences in the personality and behavior manifested by the children, which receive attention in Part II of this study. The factors in the home are the direct resultants of traits in the parents of the two compared groups, and these will be evaluated next.

Chapter III

FACTORS IN THE PERSONALITIES OF THE PARENTS

THE DISCUSSION of factors in the personalities and behavior of the parents, as they directly and indirectly affect the lives of the sex delinquents in the two compared groups, will concern itself with the items of alcoholism, drug addiction, immorality, criminality, neglect of children, periodic desertion, extreme cruelty, quarreling, and pronounced profanity.

Still other unhealthy traits in the parents, besides those listed in Table 4, may have exercised influence on the cases under study, but owing to their vague and nonmeasurable character it was not found possible to represent them statistically for analysis and interpretation.

ALCOHOLISM AND DRUG ADDICTION

Alcoholism as here understood does not connote occasionally severe or even recurrent moderate imbibition, but signifies a chronic or periodic type of drinking in which the individual loses all control of reason, balance, and concern for the welfare of himself and his family—squanders his earnings to the deprivation and distress of his dependents, invites a loss of employment through drink, abuses and assaults members of the family, employs profane language at home, causes street brawls, reaches wards of hospitals or jails, or descends to immorality. Alcoholism was found among 14.9 per cent of the mixed group fathers and 9.3 per cent of fathers in the primary group (see Table 4). There were two instances of alcoholism in mothers of the primary group, and four in the mixed group.

Healy claims[1] a finding of alcoholism among parents of 31 per cent of 1,000 repeat offenders. On the other hand, Burt

[1] Healy, W., *The Individual Delinquent*, p. 155.

33

found[2] alcoholism in only 6.5 per cent of the parents of his delinquents, and in 2.5 per cent of the parents of nondelinquents. The figures in this study are intermediate to those of Burt and Healy.

Drug addiction was found in only one parent of each group (Table 4).

TABLE 4.—*Personality Factors among Parents of Delinquents*

Type of Factor	Primary Group (108 Cases)				Mixed Group (148 Cases)			
	Father		Mother		Father		Mother	
	No.	Per-centage	No.	Per-centage	No.	Per-centage	No.	Per-centage
Alcoholism and drug addiction*	10	9.3	2	1.8	22	14.9	4	2.7
Court and jail records	4	3.7	1	0.9	12	8.1	1	0.7
Gross immorality	3	2.8	1	0.9	10	6.8	3	2.0
Neglect of children†	†	†	17	15.7	†	†	79	53.4
Desertion	11	10.2	1	0.9	16	10.8	6	4.1
Extreme cruelty	3	2.8	0	0.0	10	6.8	3	2.0
Pronounced profanity	1	0.9	0	0.0	5	3.4	1	0.7
Quarreling	7	6.4			15	10.1		
Total factors per 100 cases	36	37.0‡	20	23.7‡	61	63.0‡	65	76.3‡
Total factors per 100 cases, excluding neglect	36	37.0‡	4	26.8‡	61	63.0‡	12	73.2‡

* Drug addiction present in one father of mixed group and one mother of primary group.

† Neglect of children is arbitrarily listed in mothers' column.

‡ Percentage ratios are computed separately for the fathers in the two groups and likewise for the mothers in the two groups.

COURT AND PRISON RECORDS

This serious factor (see p. 29) in the fathers occurred more than twice as often in the mixed group as in the primary (8.1 per cent as against 3.7 per cent). The critical ratio of the difference is 1.7, and suggests some reliability. A record of this nature in a parent does not necessarily imply a permanent loss of ethics and morals, since it is not unheard of for a parent who has himself erred, to have profited sufficiently from his bitter

[2] *Op. cit.*, p. 62.

experiences to set exceptionally high standards for his offspring. In general, however, criminal court and jail experiences among parents are associated with deficiencies in personality, ethics, morals, and social views that often are morbidly reflected in the attitudes, feelings, and behavior of the children. Furthermore, in instances where a boy gains knowledge of his father's criminal record, difficulties arise for him in social adjustment, since, through his identification with his parent, ambivalent feelings of loyalty and hate lead to a consciousness of family stigma, colored by feelings of inferiority in the presence of so-considered respected members of society, and coupled with a secret distrust, hate, and vengefulness directed against all agencies of law and order. In a sensitive and impulsive child, feelings of futility, frustration, and desperation may arise, and lead to a progressively downward course. Healy lists[3] court records among the parents in 20 per cent of his cases—in 12 per cent for serious criminal or immoral acts, and in 8 per cent for minor offenses.

GROSS IMMORALITY

This was found to occur among three fathers and one mother of the primary group, as against ten fathers and three mothers of the mixed group. Immorality as here understood is not to be confused with an occasional illicit affair on the part of an indiscreet parent, a widower, or divorcee, since, if these were included, the figures in Table 4 would be many times greater. As used in this recording, the term implies a total breakdown of morals in the parents, drunken and immoral parties in the home, prostitution, paramours entertained within the home, lewd activities in the presence of the children, and degenerate practices in the home with others or upon the children.

In a closely checked study[4] of 200 delinquents and 400 nondelinquents, Burt found immorality in 2.4 per cent of parents of delinquents, against none in the control group. Burt's figures

[3] Healy and Bronner, *New Light on Juvenile Delinquency*, p. 27.
[4] *Op. cit.*, p. 62.

are generally lower than in this country, because of different conditions and sampling.

NEGLECT OF CHILDREN

The neglect of children item is based on objective data in the investigation reports of the probation officer, who makes close check on conditions in the home, in addition to gathering information from neighbors and relatives, as well as from one or the other parent and sometimes both. Neglect as here employed signifies certain character deficiencies in the parents that serve to deprive the children of reasonable care, training, and guidance, as found in homes where alcoholism and vice are rampant, homes with immoral and psychopathic parents, with mentally or physically incompetent, feebleminded, or indifferent parents, homes with ignorant and hostile step-parents, etc.

Neglect of children was found, as shown in Table 4, to occur among 53.4 per cent of the mixed group cases and 15.7 per cent of the primary. The item may be regarded as an important factor in the lives of the delinquents, since it occurs more than three times as often in the mixed group as in the primary. The critical ratio of the difference is equal to 6.9, which is highly reliable.

Healy and Bronner found[5] that 22 per cent of a series of 4,000 juvenile delinquents suffered from extreme parental neglect.

Neglect of children is listed under the mothers' column in the table, not because the father bears no blame, but rather because the mother is more closely identified with the routine care and guidance of the children, and because any attempt at statistical segregation of this item, as between fathers and mothers, would prove arbitrary and misleading.

DESERTION

Periodic desertion of home and family by fathers appears with almost equal frequency in the primary and mixed groups

[5] *Delinquents and Criminals*, p. 125.

(10.2 per cent versus 10.8 per cent); hence it is apparently not a factor in the behavior and prospects of the children.

Desertion on the part of the mothers is found in six instances in the mixed group, as against one in the primary group (Table 4). Desertion is more significant when it is the mother's defection, since it is productive of greater repercussions in the feelings and behavior of the offspring.

EXTREME CRUELTY

The item is listed in Table 4 only in instances where there is a record of actual morbid action on the part of a parent toward a child, such as tying a child to a pole, locking him in a cellar overnight, brutal physical discipline, violence toward a child while under the influence of drink, or cruelty occasioned by mental illness in a parent or hostility in a step-parent. It is found almost three times as often among fathers of the mixed group as among those of the primary (6.8 per cent as against 2.8 per cent). It is of interest to note that of the ten fathers so listed in the mixed group, six were chronic alcoholics, and one was an epileptic.

No instance of cruelty was found among the mothers in the primary group, and only three instances were present among mothers in the mixed group; two of these mothers were alcoholic and the other psychopathically immoral.

Kempf comments on cruel parents thus: "Most of our chronic lawbreakers and asocial adults, thieves, pimps, and prostitutes, whether mental defectives or not, are chronically asocial in their tendencies, because of the pernicious influence of mismated parents or the hatred of the adults who raised them."[6]

QUARRELING BETWEEN PARENTS

This represents more or less continual conflict between parents of a type serious enough to affect the sense of well-being and security of the children. The data are derived from pro-

[6] *Op. cit.*, p. 104.

bation officers' investigations. The item is found to exist in 10.1 per cent of the mixed group homes and in 6.4 per cent of the primary, as shown in Table 4. Healy reports[7] quarreling of a serious nature in 12 per cent of the homes of delinquents.

PRONOUNCED PROFANITY

Only instances of habitual uncontrolled obscenity, of a type likely to injure the moral fiber of a child, are included in Table 4. While the incidence is small, the total force of many such defects nevertheless adds up to a rather imposing picture of unhealthy parental influences, as will be noted in the summary.

SUMMARY

The outstanding defects among primary group fathers are alcoholism and desertion, whereas in the mixed group are found alcoholism, desertion, criminality, immorality, and cruelty. Table 4 reveals a total of 36 personality defects per 100 of the primary group fathers, as compared with 61 for the mixed group. This corresponds to a ratio of 37 per cent among primary group fathers and to 63 per cent among mixed group fathers, with a critical ratio of the difference equal to 3.7, which reflects true reliability.

On the score of total character defects, the ratio is 76.3 per cent for the mixed group mothers, as compared with only 23.7 per cent for the primary group mothers. The critical ratio of this difference is 7.2, which indicates high reliability.

When fathers and mothers are compared, there is a much greater frequency of character defects in the former than in the latter with the neglect item omitted. The neglect item is recorded in the mothers' column, not because the fathers are absolved of blame, but merely because it was not possible to distribute the scoring accurately among mothers and fathers, and because the mothers are closer to the home and children.

[7] Healy and Bronner, *op. cit.*, p. 129.

Thus, the primary group ratio of defects, in a comparison of fathers to mothers per 100 cases, is 36:4, and in the mixed group 61:12. The ready implication of the difference is that the mothers, as a sampling, are constituted of better personality material than the fathers, and that the primary group mothers far surpass the mixed group mothers in character make-up.

Summing up the defects of fathers and mothers in each group, one finds twice the number of parental factors in the mixed group as compared with the primary. Furthermore, not only are the unfavorable parental traits decisively balanced against the prospects of the children in the mixed group, but the favorable factors of home and family life (see chap. ii) are significantly wanting among the children of this group.

The differences in the tangible home and parental factors between the general delinquents of the mixed group and the true sex offenders of the primary group are pronounced, being supported by a critical ratio of difference varying from 3 to 7. These, when taken in conjunction with nonmeasurable factors (chap. ii, summary), provide an impressive picture of the abnormal conditions operating in the backgrounds of mixed group delinquents that are likely to find reflection in their response to community conditions and in their personality traits, which will be discussed in succeeding chapters. The significance of such conditionings in the evolution of the general delinquent is stressed by the Gluecks thus: "The important point is that a family tradition of lawlessness and vice, and the attitudes evolved in the homes where such lawlessness and vice are common experiences, are not conducive to a habit of mind and behavior that ordinarily makes for decent citizenship."[8]

[8] *500 Criminal Careers*, p. 112.

Chapter IV

COMMUNITY FACTORS

THE FACTORS of home and parents have received attention. To complete the analysis of the background, the factors deriving from community relationships will be considered as concerns the two compared groups. Neighborhood factors bear significantly on the nature and development of a child, particularly in sections where homes are poorly organized, controls and supervision lacking, and the children are left more or less continually to the pressure of the morbid and antisocial currents of "the street."

BAD NEIGHBORHOOD

Data regarding this item are derived from information in probation officers' investigation records, which in turn is based on established ratings of morbidity of certain segments of New York City. Table 5 shows 52.8 per cent of the mixed group cases and 35.1 per cent of the primary as living in bad neighborhoods, with a critical ratio of the difference equal to 2.8, which denotes reliability. In cosmopolitan life, with its crowded slum and gang-ridden areas, children who are entirely abandoned to their own resources find it most difficult to retain and maintain decent viewpoints and behavior. There is often a sharp struggle for survival against the continual onslaughts of aggressive and antisocial types. Resistance to the gang means not only risk of bodily harm and abuse, but also exclusion from games and neighborhood activities, and hence requires an exceptional amount of individual fortitude.

Boys are not infrequently compelled to face such situations against great odds, either because shame and pride prevent them from turning to parents and guardians for assistance, or because some parents are known to tell their children, if they complain of difficulties with "tough" boys, to "fight their own battles." Thus many children who intrinsically detest the ideologies and behavior of delinquent types, nevertheless eventually, through pressure, are forced to accept these conditions

TABLE 5.—*Community Factors Affecting Primary and Mixed Group Delinquents**

Type of Factor	Primary Group 108 Cases		Mixed Group 148 Cases		Total 256 Cases	
	No. of Cases	Per-centage	No. of Cases	Per-centage	No. of Cases	Per-centage
Bad neighborhood	38	35.1	78	52.8	126	45.3
Bad company (gang)	2	1.8	39	26.3	41	16.0
Excess movies	4	3.7	13	8.8	17	6.7
Demoralizing recreation	1	0.9	16	10.8	17	6.7
Chronic late hours	0	0.0	47	31.7	47	18.4
School maladjustment	5	4.6	109	73.6	114	44.6
Occasional or no church attendance	43	39.8	90	61.0	133	52.0
Hazardous vocations	1	0.9	8	5.4	9	3.5
Total factors per 100 cases	87	24.3	270	75.7		

* More than one factor is listed per case.

for protection and security. They become warped in personality, so that they soon become indistinguishable from the others, and in turn serve to drag still others down to this level.

But why do these young men want to persuade you? Because they desire to seduce you; they do not care for you, they take no real interest in you; their only motive is a secret spite because they see that you are better than they; they want to drag you down to their own level. Do you think you have anything to gain by this? Are they so much wiser than I? Is the affection of a day stronger than mine?[1]

The fact, however, that 35 per cent of the primary group children were exposed to these so-called bad neighborhoods and yet managed to be free of the general delinquent traits of the mixed group, such as burglarly, robbery, etc., would imply that neighborhood factors, per se, are not invariable determinants

[1] Rousseau, J. J., *Emile*, p. 297.

of a child's behavior, provided favorable home conditions exist to counterbalance their effects.

GANGS AND BAD COMPANY

The gang factor was found to operate among 26.3 per cent of the mixed group cases, and in only 1.8 per cent of the primary (Table 5). This difference is of signal importance, considering that the ratio of bad neighborhoods in the two groups was no greater than that of 52 per cent to 35 per cent. Factors of home (p. 32) rather than neighborhood may therefore be assumed to account for the difference. One must conjecture a sharp dissimilarity in attitudes, behavior, and ideation among the boys of the two groups, as they either accepted or rejected the friendships and standards of the gang type. It is recognized that not all gangs are directed toward delinquent or destructive behavior, but most of those operating in slum areas become so from time to time. The gang, as constituted in the poor, disorganized neighborhoods, may engage in games or athletics one minute and turn to holdups or stealing the next minute. In this connection, Thrasher says:

The present study does not advance the thesis that the gang is a "cause" of crime. It would be more accurate to say that the gang is an important contributing factor, facilitating the commission of crime and greatly extending its spread and range. . . . The boy in the gang learns the technique of crime by observing it in older boys. . . . Exact information as to the technique of crime is imparted in the gang. Experience in a gang of the predatory type usually develops in the boy an attitude of indifference to law and order—one of the basic traits of the finished gangster. . . . The gang boy very early acquires the independence which is characteristic of the finished gangster—learns to sleep away from home and live on his own (predatory resources). . . . The boy usually acquires in the gang an attitude of fatalism, a willingness to take a chance—a philosophy of life which fits him well for a career of crime.[2]

[2] Thrasher, F. M., *The Gang*, pp. 381–392.

Burt reveals[3] bad companionship (including gangs) to exist in 23.6 per cent of delinquents, and in only 1 per cent of nondelinquents. Note needs to be taken of the remarkably close resemblance of Burt's figures to those for the mixed and primary groups, respectively, the former group consisting of general delinquents involved also in sex offenses, and the primary group being involved in no known offenses other than sexual.

Healy and Bronner make claim[4] to a finding of 62 per cent for bad company (including gangs) among 3,000 delinquents, which is considerably higher than the percentage found in this study, and yet serves to reflect the morbidity of certain environments.

Types of play and play roles appearing among the delinquents are listed in Tables 34 and 35 of the Appendix.

EXCESSIVE MOTION PICTURE ATTENDANCE

Movie attendance among the delinquents is listed as excessive only where evidence is recorded, on complaint of parents or admissions of the boy, that movies were visited three or more times a week. This condition was found to exist among 8.8 per cent of the cases in the mixed group and in 3.7 per cent of the primary group cases (see Table 5). The exact significance of this item is not clear without available detailed knowledge as to the type of cinema, the boys' reactions to the picture, etc. Burt finds[5] movies a factor in 7 per cent of his delinquents.

Excessive motion picture attendance is found in 55 per cent of delinquents by Healy and Bronner.[6] These figures are somewhat high and are no doubt occasioned by a different criterion of "excessive attendance," yet cognizance should be taken of the disorganized general behavior of delinquent boys—that they play truant and employ their lunch money for movies, visit movies with the gang, desert home, and invariably find

[3] *Op. cit.,* p. 125.
[4] *Op. cit.,* p. 179.
[5] *Op. cit.,* p. 137.
[6] *New Light on Juvenile Delinquency,* p. 53.

their way into movies through one means or another; the proceeds of all stealing ventures go largely to movie fare. In some boys the factor very likely operates as a demoralizing recreational activity.

DEMORALIZING RECREATION

This item includes unhealthy recreation of children, such as visiting pool rooms, penny arcades, gambling places, public dance halls, unsupervised parties, houses of prostitution, and the like. These unhealthy interests frequently flow from the influence of bad company. Demoralizing recreational activities occurred with a frequency of 10.8 per cent in the mixed group, as compared with only 0.9 per cent in the primary group (see Table 5). Healy and Bronner[7] found 20 per cent of their delinquents participating in poor types of recreation.

HABITUAL LATE HOURS

The condition was found to exist with the appalling frequency of 31.7 per cent in the mixed group cases, as against none recorded for the primary group (see Table 5). This is not to be interpreted to signify that no member of the primary group ever remained out late at night, but that as an item of regular practice, against the wishes of the parents, no such instances were found. The great frequency of this very objectionable trait among the children of the mixed group can only denote that they were completely beyond the control of their parents, or that their parents were so deficient in character and social responsibility as to be totally indifferent or oblivious to such behavior on the part of their offspring. Late hours, like unhealthy types of recreation, usually spring from the influence of evil companions.

SCHOOL MALADJUSTMENT

Maladjustment, as listed in Table 5, does not refer to instances of petty misbehavior on the part of a child, or to an

[7] *Delinquents and Criminals*, p. 181.

occasional infraction of school regulations. It represents a situation in which a child is in complete rebellion against and disharmony with the school system, in continual defiance of law and order in the classroom, and beyond the control of different teachers in successive attempts to readapt him to the requirements of school discipline and program. Maladjustment at school is found among 73.6 per cent of the mixed group cases, as against only 4.6 per cent of the primary group (Diagram 5).

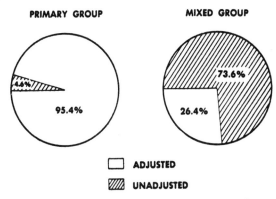

DIAGRAM 5. SCHOOL ADJUSTMENT OF BOY SEX OFFENDERS OF PRIMARY AND OF MIXED GROUP

The deplorably high frequency of school maladjustment among three-fourths of the mixed group population may be considered a potent force for evil, albeit it is recognized that this is but one of many symptoms of behavior disorganization among these children (late hours, gang activities, demoralizing recreation, and general-delinquent habits). One can readily appreciate that a boy who is totally beyond the control of his family and hostile toward society, because of antisocial and gang ideologies, will automatically resist, defy, and obstruct the orderly processes of the classroom, and constitute a problem and often a menace to the school. Healy and Bronner[8]

[8] *New Light on Juvenile Delinquency*, p. 53.

find 40 per cent of delinquents showing a strong dislike for school.

OCCASIONAL OR NO CHURCH ATTENDANCE

This item was found among 61 per cent of mixed group cases, for all religious denominations, as against 39.8 per cent of the primary group (Table 5). The true reliability of this difference is reflected in the critical ratio of 3.4. The lack of spiritual influence among more than half of the total number of cases is disturbing, although it is difficult to gauge the frequency in the general population, for comparative statistics, owing to a lack of reliable data and the fragmentary and inadequate samplings.[9] The findings reflect the negligence or indifference of the parents, and, in the mixed group, may in addition be related to the fact that these children, through aggressiveness, have broken away from family controls. Table 36 (Appendix) reveals almost similar distributions regarding church attendance among the various religious faiths.

Payne offers his views on causes of delinquency: "Many of the social phenomena of the twentieth century, such as crime, may be traced directly to the break-down of the old authority of the family, the church, and the school, and the failure to substitute in their place adequate controls within the individual."[10]

HAZARDOUS VOCATIONAL INTERESTS

This factor accounts for 5.4 per cent of cases in the mixed group as against 0.9 per cent in the primary group (Table 5). It concerns such unhealthy vocational practices as selling newspapers throughout the night, shoe shining or entertaining in grills, saloons, and night clubs, etc.

[9] The Gluecks comment on this circumstance as follows: "The absence of reliable comparable data regarding the nondelinquents does not, however, as some have inferred, vitiate all research into the make-up of delinquents": *One Thousand Juvenile Delinquents,* p. 63.

[10] Payne, E. G., *Principles of Educational Psychology,* p. 123.

SUMMARY

Damaging community factors are found in 270 instances per 100 cases of the mixed group juveniles, and in 87 instances of the primary group, or in 75.7 per cent of the former as against 24.3 per cent of the latter. The difference is highly reliable, being supported by a critical ratio of 8.3.

Moreover, the most unhealthy factors growing from community experiences (i.e., participation in gangs, demoralizing recreation, habitual late hours, and school maladjustment), occur from *ten to thirty times* as frequently in the mixed group as in the primary.

Furthermore, while counterbalancing favorable home factors (p. 32) serve to offset the small damage of the community factors in the primary group, comparatively few such advantages exist within the homes of the mixed group members. Some indication of the operation of strengthening forces in the primary group homes is afforded by the finding that, although *35 per cent* of primary group boys were submerged in neighborhoods classified as definitely "bad," *only 1 per cent* of the group became involved in "gangs." On the other hand, *52 per cent* of the mixed group cases were located in such neighborhoods, and *26 per cent* of the group participated in "gangs."

Habitual late hours, found among 31.7 per cent of the mixed group cases, as compared with none in the primary group, serve to reflect either a complete breakdown of parental control or total indifference among the parents as to the conduct of their offspring. As the children become mature enough to step out of the home, their responses and adaptations to community situations reveal in type and gravity the particular conditionings effected by the parents. The pronounced differences noted above in the two groups with regard to the factors of gang participation and late hours, even with due allowance for special community stresses, afford ample evidence for the indictment of the homes (chap. ii, summary) and parents (chap. iii, summary) of the mixed group, as the immediate responsible agents in the wretched showing of their children.

The significant factors of late hours, demoralizing recreation, and gang participation appear to be strong precursors of school maladjustment; and these four behavior abnormalities are probably *the most potent determinants of the general offenses, common to all members of the mixed group,* on the basis of which they were originally segregated from the primary. *These four salient factors* are also likely to appear significantly reflected in the personality abnormalities and outcomes of mixed group members, in comparison with primary, which will be dealt with in succeeding chapters.

PART II

PERSONALITY OF THE SEX DELINQUENT

PRECEDING sections of the study have dealt with the background of the two compared types of sex delinquents. Group analyses were employed to establish factors in the parents, home, and neighborhood, that were likely to bear on the personality and behavior of the children, in the light of later outcomes.

This part of the investigation will concern itself with a breakdown of the elements in the personalities of members of the two compared juvenile groups, in order to establish differences that might stand in relation to the background forces and the later life outcomes. A working definition of personality would be that it comprises the sum total of a boy's inherent traits, his experiences, temperament traits, and behavior. The following items will receive attention: inherent traits among the compared sex delinquents (chap. v); disorders of body and mind (chap. vi); disorders in temperament and behavior (chap. vii); types of offenses committed by the two groups (chap. viii)— (a) sex nature of the offenses, (b) the offender's role, (c) the causes, (d) offenses other than sexual, (e) court and clinic treatment of the offenders.

Chapter V

INHERENT TRAITS

<small>T</small>HE TRAITS of age, race, nationality, religion, and intelligence are submitted for orientation as to the make-up of the sampling of boys in the two compared groups.

<small>AGE DISTRIBUTION AND PUBERTY</small>

It is interesting to note, in Diagram 6 and Table 37 (Appendix), the uniform distribution of cases in the two groups at the different age levels. As an instance, in the 7- to 14-year age range there are 47 per cent primary and 46.7 per cent mixed group cases. The mean figures of the ages again show close correspondence in the two groups, with 13.7 years for the primary and 13.5 years for the mixed group. The age used is as of the boy's last birthday.

Table 38 (Appendix) will be found to reveal a greater incidence of mixed group cases at age levels below puberty (25.7 per cent for the mixed as against 16.6 per cent for the primary group). The difference might be attributable to greater disorganization in mixed group homes (chap. ii), and greater neglect of children (chap. iii), which permit these youngsters to roam the streets unsupervised, a ready prey to scheming degenerate elements in the milieu. The mean of the puberty ages for members of both groups was 12.4 years. Puberty brings about an activity of the sex glands that heightens the imagination, excites the emotional and bodily states, arouses sacral autonomic cravings, and contributes to the commission of sex offenses. Thus, 83.4 per cent of the primary group and 74.3 per cent of the mixed group sex offenders were past puberty, i.e., were early adolescents.

<small>RACE</small>

For data and discussion of race among the delinquents, reference should be made to page 19, and Diagram 2, for in all instances the race of the delinquent was the same as that of the parents.

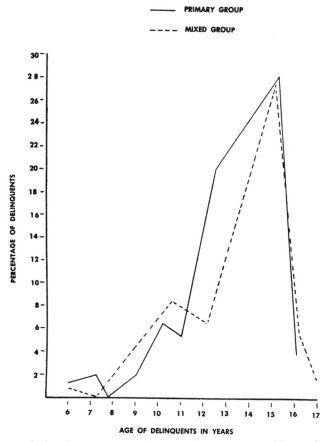

DIAGRAM 6. AGE DISTRIBUTION OF BOYS OF PRIMARY AND OF MIXED GROUP

NATIONALITY

Nationality shows little variation in the two groups. Native delinquents constitute 93.6 per cent of the primary and 95.6 per cent of the mixed group. Foreign-born delinquents account for 6.4 per cent of primary and 4.1 per cent of mixed group cases, as shown in Table 23 of the Appendix and Diagram 7.

The small percentage of foreign-born delinquents in the series (5 per cent) is in sharp contrast to the very large percentage (60 per cent) of foreign-born parents (see p. 20). There is implication of marked differences in cultural patterns, language, and customs as between the parents and children, and yet, since the frequencies in the two groups are fairly

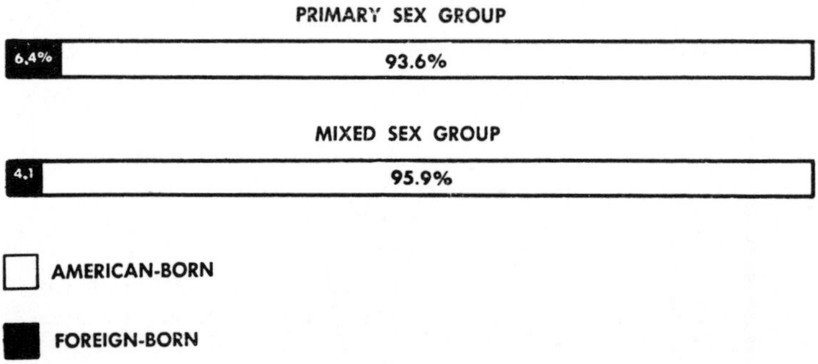

PRIMARY SEX GROUP

6.4%	93.6%

MIXED SEX GROUP

4.1	95.9%

☐ AMERICAN-BORN

■ FOREIGN-BORN

DIAGRAM 7. NATIONALITY DISTRIBUTION OF PRIMARY AND MIXED GROUP DELINQUENTS

uniform, no significant import may be expected from the trait of nationality for the purposes of this study (see p. 20).

RELIGION

The particular faith of a child (Table 39, Appendix) appears not to operate as a factor in one group as compared with the other, since there is an almost even distribution of the different religions among the primary and mixed group members (Catholics, 50 per cent of the primary group and 52.7 per cent of the mixed; Protestants, 28.7 per cent of the primary and 29.7 per cent of the mixed group; and Jews, 21.3 per cent of the primary and 17.6 per cent of the mixed group).

INTELLIGENCE

The intelligence ratings are based on the Stanford-Binet standardized tests, although performance in other psychometric tests is given due consideration.

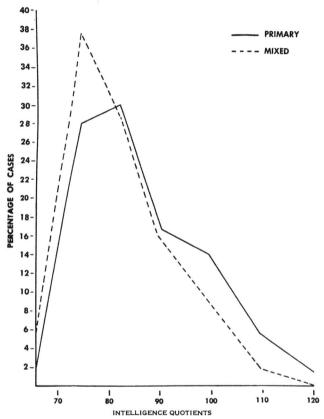

DIAGRAM 8. INTELLIGENCE DISTRIBUTION OF JUVENILE SEX DELINQUENTS OF PRIMARY AND OF MIXED GROUP

Differences in the two groups on the score of native intelligence are small (see Diagram 8 and Table 6), and hence appear not to operate as a factor in terms of outcomes. A small number of cases falling below the 70 I.Q. level (9 in all, or 3.5

per cent of the entire series) are included in the study, because other indications prompted the psychologist and psychiatrist to believe that these exceptional cases were not truly feeble-minded. The mixed group members appear to employ native intelligence to less advantage than the primary group members, as shown by the grade advancement of children of similar mental ages (see Table 40).

TABLE 6.—*Intelligence Distribution among Delinquents of Primary and Mixed Groups*

Range of Intelligence Quotient	Primary Group (108 Cases)		Mixed Group (148 Cases)		Total (256 Cases)	
	No.	Percentage	No.	Percentage	No.	Percentage
120+	2	1.8	0	0.0	2	0.8
110–120	6	5.5	3	2.0	9	3.5
100–110	15	13.9	15	10.1	30	11.7
90–100	18	16.6	24	16.3	42	16.4
80–90	33	30.6	42	28.4	75	29.3
70–80	30	27.8	55	37.2	85	33.2
60–70	2	1.8	7	4.7	9	3.5
Unknown	2	1.8	2	1.3	4	1.6
Total	108	100.0	148	100.0	256	100.0

SUMMARY

The inherent attributes of age, race, religion, nationality, and intelligence are fairly evenly distributed in the two groups. These characteristics have been presented not with the thought of disclosing probable sharp differences as factors in relation to the outcomes, but rather for a fuller understanding of the make-up of the two compared samplings of cases. Of passing interest, however, are the findings that only one-fifth of the entire series of sexual offenders fall below the puberty or adolescent age level, and that grade advancement among members of the two groups with similar mental ages makes a better showing in the primary group.

Chapter VI

DISORDERS OF BODY AND MIND

OUR NEXT step is the evaluation of salient differences in the mental, emotional, and behavior traits among members of the two compared groups, both as end products of the background conditioning processes and as factors in relation to the later outcomes. The physical disorders, being natural phenomena, are presented for completion of the personality picture, and not because they necessarily stem from background influences.

PHYSICAL DISORDERS

The physical disorders recorded in Table 7 are of a serious nature, including partial blindness, deafness, body deformities, tuberculosis, severe heart ailments, and marked malnutrition. Mild physical deviations are not considered here, since there is scarcely a child who has not at some time or other suffered from some minor physical ailment. In this connection, Healy and Bronner note[1] the insignificance of minor ailments in relation to the behavior patterns and life course of a child. Ira Wile states: "There is too free a tendency to seize upon a physical fact as sufficient to account for all the difficulties of childhood, without correlations with the other elements of the personality."[2]

Serious physical defects occur in 11.1 per cent of primary group cases and 3.4 per cent of mixed group cases, showing a critical ratio of difference of 2.3, which is below reliability. There is, nevertheless, indication that a larger segment of the primary than of the mixed group is possessed of poor physical structure. Healy[3] notes that poor physical make-up is one

[1] *Op. cit.*, chap. v.
[2] *Op. cit.*, p. 60.
[3] Healy and Bronner, *op. cit.*, chap. iv.

of the conditions preventing some children from engaging in aggressive delinquent conduct, such as hitching on cars, desertion of home, robbery, etc.   The primary group by definition consists of children who had not engaged in any delinquent behavior other than sexual, and this in small part may be attributed to physical infirmity.

Glandular Disorders. The glandular defects are minor deviations, few in number, and distributed about equally in the two groups.   Glandular or endocrine disturbances have been unwarrantedly emphasized as basic determinants of all types

TABLE 7.—*Physical Disorders among the Delinquents*

Type of Disorder	Primary Group 108 Cases		Mixed Group 148 Cases		Total 256 Cases	
	No. of Cases	Per-centage	No. of Cases	Per-centage	No. of Cases	Per-centage
Serious physical defects	12	11.1	5	3.4	17	6.7
Glandular (endocrine) defects (over- or underfunctioning; over- or under-development)	5	4.6	6	4.1	11	4.3
Total defects per 100 cases	15	67.7*	7	32.3*		

* Percentages for total defects are calculated on the basis of the sum of the factors in the two groups per 100 cases; however, the number of defects per 100 cases is so small that the percentage ratios are not actually significant (CR is only 2.3).

of delinquency by some writers, especially Schlapp,[4] who devoted an entire volume to the subject, with photographs, measurements of arm to body ratio, and elaborate attempts at glandular interpretation of microscopic physical variations among children that are naturally and normally to be expected even among healthiest specimens (see p. 13).   The finding of so small an incidence of glandular defects, particularly in a series of sexual offenders, clearly enough indicates that delinquency and criminality, sexual or general, do not derive from this source.

[4] Schlapp, M., and Smith, E. H., *The New Criminology.*

NERVOUS AND MENTAL DISORDERS

The diagnosis of a nervous or mental disorder is based on a thorough study of the past behavior of the boy, his emotional reactions during the examination, and the content of his mind. It rests on determinations of whether the boy expresses delusions of persecution, or hallucinations; whether he is seriously disturbed emotionally; whether he presents bizarre behavior patterns; whether there is a history of convulsions, serious head injury, or congenital syphilis; whether there is a morbid outlook

TABLE 8.—*Nervous and Mental Disorders among the Delinquents*

Type of Disorder	Primary Group 108 Cases		Mixed Group 148 Cases		Total 256 Cases	
	No. of Cases	Per-centage	No. of Cases	Per-centage	No. of Cases	Per-centage
Psychotic	2	1.8	7	4.7	9	3.5
Post-traumatic	1	0.9	2	1.3	3	1.2
Epileptic	3	2.8	1	0.7	4	1.6
Postencephalitic	0	0.0	2	1.3	2	0.8
Postchoreic	0	0.0	1	0.7	1	0.4
Congenital syphilitic	0	0.0	1	0.7	1	0.4
Psychopathic	4	3.7	18	12.2	22	8.6
Neurotic	18	16.6	37	25.0	55	21.5
Unstable	7	6.4	35	23.6	42	16.4
Total disorders per 100 cases	32	31.5†	70	68.5†		

* Only one disorder listed for any case.
† Percentages calculated on the basis of total disorders in the two groups per 100 cases.

toward life, or a paranoid-psychopathic attitude toward society. (As previously stated, cases of feeblemindedness are excluded from the investigation.)

Psychopathic personality may be roughly defined as a morbid type of personality, with strong antisocial leanings and a rebelliousness against social conventions and regulations. Neurotic personality signifies an inability to solve an internal conflict or complex, such as occurs from an abnormal attachment to a parent, a fear of bodily harm through excessive narcissism, etc. Unstable personality denotes a state of maladjustment deriving from personal, social, sexual, or physical factors.

Table 8 reveals 32 instances of nervous and mental disorders per 100 cases of the primary group, to 70 such instances per 100 cases of the mixed group, or a ratio of 31.5 per cent in the primary group, to 68.5 per cent in the mixed group. The critical ratio of the difference in the two groups is 5.6, which reflects high reliability.

The differences in the two groups on the score of posttraumatic, epileptic, postencephalitic, postchoreic, and syphilitic nervous disorders are negligible. On the score of *psychopathic, psychotic*, and *unstable personality*, however, pronounced differences appear in the two groups, with almost four times as many instances among members of the mixed group as among the primary. Nervous and mental disorders are therefore to be considered as probable factors bearing on the outcomes in the two groups.

SUMMARY

The incidence of serious physical infirmity among the sex delinquents is small (6.7 per cent of the entire series). Although there is a comparatively greater frequency in the primary group than in the mixed, the critical ratio of difference is 2.3, which is below reliability. Mild physical ailments bear little relation to the welfare or behavior of children and are therefore not considered in Table 7. Glandular disorders are of mild type, occur in only 4 per cent of the cases, are evenly distributed in the two groups, and palpably bear no relationship to the origin of either sexual or general forms of delinquency.

Mental and nervous disorders are found to occur more than twice as often among members of the mixed group as of the primary. Of the factors of *psychopathic, psychotic*, and *unstable personality*, there are four times as many instances in the mixed group, and these may have strong bearing on the outcomes in the two compared groups.

Hirsch states: "In at least 65 per cent of our cases [i.e., general delinquents] a major abnormality exists, of either intellect or the personality.   This percentage of deviation is probably from four and a half to five times as great as is found in the population at large."[5]

On the basis of personality abnormalities, Hirsch's delinquents correspond closely to our mixed group general-delinquent cases.   In the same ratio and on the same basis the primary group cases correspond to nondelinquents in the general population (see also p. 43).   However, on the score abnormality of intellect, this study does not support Hirsch's data, since no essential differences appear between the mixed and primary groups (see p. 53).

[5] *Op. cit.*, p. 60.

Chapter VII

DISORDERS IN TEMPERAMENT AND BEHAVIOR

DISORDERS IN TEMPERAMENT

IT IS planned to treat separately the disorders of temperament and behavior, although it is realized that in certain
respects no sharp demarcation exists between them, since very
often one condition occasions or is associated with the other.
Furthermore, it is recognized that a particular temperament
manifestation is not a permanent feature in a child, but may
come and go. Yet temperament represents an affective pattern in the child and is attached to a large segment of the
personality, ideation, and feelings, as distinguished from
emotion, which is a fleeting state of feeling response to a
stimulus or situation.

Restlessness (Excitability).[1] This trait occurs among 73.7
per cent of mixed group cases, as against only 8.3 per cent of
primary group cases (Table 9). The finding that three-fourths
of the mixed group population are so disturbed in temperament
may be considered as reflecting a potent cause of their marked
antisocial conduct and their general maladjustment at home,
at school, and in the community. In part, however, the item
may be the result of such uncontrollable and offensive behavior.
As cause or result, the trait of restlessness bears close relationship to the unhealthy behavior of the mixed group children,
constitutes a salient item differentiating the mixed group
boy from the primary, and should probably operate as a major
factor in the outcomes.

---

[1] Healy and Bronner find the following among 153 carefully studied delinquents: overrestlessness and overactivity, 34 per cent of the cases; tempers
and irritability, 28 per cent: *op. cit.*, p. 53.

Instances of restlessness among mixed group cases are as follows:

Case 110. Age, 13. Bully, rebellious at home and school, ungovernable, keeps late hours; nail biting, pilfering, desertion; forced sodomy on small boy.

Case 199. Age, 13. Confirmed school problem, gambles, keeps late hours, stutters, bullies, is ungovernable, and uses vulgar language

TABLE 9.—*Temperament Disorders among the Delinquents**

Type of Disorder	Primary Group 108 Cases		Mixed Group 148 Cases		Total 256 Cases	
	No. of Cases	Per-centage	No. of Cases	Per-centage	No. of Cases	Per-centage
Restlessness (excitability)	9	8.3	109	73.7	118	46.1
Stubbornness	7	6.4	72	48.7	79	30.8
Aggressiveness	10	9.2	63	42.5	73	28.6
Timidity (docility)	34	31.4	20	13.5	54	21.1
Surliness (irritability)	2	1.8	23	15.5	25	9.8
Apathy	8	7.4	3	2.0	11	4.3
Moodiness	8	7.4	14	9.5	22	8.6
Jealousy	1	0.9	5	3.4	6	2.3
Callousness	0	0.0	9	6.1	9	3.5
Cruelty	1	0.9	18	12.2	19	7.4
Total disorders per 100 cases	74	26.6†	227	75.4†		

* More than one disorder listed for some of the cases.

† Percentages calculated on the basis of the sum of the disorders in the two groups per 100 cases.

at home; threatened to kill his father; enuretic, rebellious, excitable; made sex attempt with little girl.

Case 212. Age, 14. Untidy, truant, destructive, lies, keeps late hours, steals everything in sight, fights at home, throws bottles from roof at children; attacked several little girls.

Case 215. Age, 10. Wild, untidy, dirty, enuretic, destructive, uncontrollable at school and home; made sex attempt with sister.

Case 222. Age, 12. Truant, maladjusted at school, bully, aggressive, smokes, keeps late hours; rebellious at home, stubborn, impulsive, violent, defiant, pulls mother's hair, breaks windows, has tempers, uses wild language to mother, steals, deserts; practiced sodomy with adults, made sodomy attempt on younger brother, etc.

Stubbornness. This unhealthy trait is found among 48.7 per cent of the mixed group cases, and in only 6.4 per cent of the primary group. Such difference in frequency is significant both for the juvenile and later life behavior of the two compared groups.

Aggressiveness. This is found among 42.5 per cent of the mixed group cases, as against 9.2 per cent of the primary group. The triad of *restlessness, stubbornness,* and *aggressiveness* occurs from *five to ten times as frequently in the mixed group* as in the primary. The differences carry high reliability, since they are supported by a critical ratio of difference of 9.0. These traits are very likely the most salient determinants of general delinquency among mixed group boys, and should be reflected as major factors in the outcomes.

Timidity (Docility). This temperament pattern, which covers shyness as well, is found to a much greater extent in the primary than in the mixed group (31.4 per cent as against 13.5 per cent). The reliability of the difference is supported by a critical ratio of 3.4. While this item cannot be considered favorable or desirable, it may nevertheless be assumed that, since of all the unhealthy temperament traits this alone is found predominantly in the primary group, it is probably not a serious drawback to a boy's progress or social adjustment. The sum of the findings, thus far, supports the conviction that timid children, as a group, do not constitute poor prospective material.

Surliness. This is found to exist among 15.5 per cent of the mixed group children, as compared with 1.8 per cent of the primary group. The critical ratio of the difference is 4.3, a figure of definite reliability. A surly temperament reflects a rather morbid turn in a boy's personality, and is associated with an attitude of smugness and indifference toward the orderly processes of society and its institutions. It is often a forerunner of a paranoid state of mind in later years.

Apathy. This occurs in only 8 cases of the primary group and 3 of the mixed group, and is apparently of no signal importance in the general behavior of either group of boys.

Moodiness. Found in 9.5 per cent of the mixed group and 7.4 per cent of the primary group boys, this is similarly not of weighty significance.

Callousness. This is found among 6.1 per cent of the mixed group cases, and not at all in the primary group. However, the trait denotes such pronounced morbidity in the feelings and conduct of a boy with regard to ethics, morals, and family ties, that it warrants consideration as a factor, despite its small incidence. The most flagrant and vicious violators of the social codes, manifesting no concern as to consequence or conscience, are found in this category.

Cruelty. This trait is found among 12.2 per cent of the offenders of the mixed group, while only one such instance is recorded in the primary group. It denotes a severe type of morbidity that warrants consideration as a possible factor.

BEHAVIOR DISORDERS

Almost every behavior disorder, if reduced to its roots, could be traced to faulty conditioning in the home or neighborhood. Some behavior defects, such as nail biting, are comparatively mild, while others, such as bed wetting and speech disorders, are deeply allied to disorganization in the personality. Some behavior traits are readily amenable to remedy, while others are very difficult to eradicate, particularly if associated with unhealthy temperament traits of excitability, instability, and stubbornness.

A group of salient behavior disorders, not listed in Table 10, including late hours, demoralizing recreation, school maladjustment, and gang activity, have received attention under the subject of community factors (see summary, chap. iv), and are therefore not reincluded here, but will be given due consideration in later summary evaluations of juvenile behavior disorders.

Gambling. This is found among 9.5 per cent of cases in the mixed group, as compared with 1.8 per cent in the primary group. There is a true difference in the critical ratio of 2.9. All children at times gamble with tickets or a few pennies;

TABLE 10.—*Behavior Abnormalities among the Delinquents**

Type of Behavior Disorder	Primary Group 108 Cases		Mixed Group 148 Cases		Total 256 Cases	
	No. of Cases	Per-centage	No. of Cases	Per-centage	No. of Cases	Per-centage
Gambling	2	1.8	14	9.5	16	6.3
Smoking (excessive)	5	4.6	16	10.8	21	8.2
Alcoholism (use of intoxicants)	0	0.0	11	7.4	11	4.3
Delinquency habit	0	0.0	26	17.6	26	10.2
Enuresis	19	17.6	34	23.0	53	20.7
Soiling	1	0.9	1	0.7	2	0.8
Nail biting	7	6.4	20	13.5	27	10.6
Face or head tics	1	0.9	6	4.1	7	2.7
Sleep walking, sleep talking	3	2.8	23	15.5	26	10.2
Sleeping with mother or sister	3	2.8	4	2.7	7	2.7
Nightmares	0	0.0	3	2.0	3	1.2
Fear of dark	1	0.9	3	2.0	4	1.6
Effeminacy ("sissy" behavior)	6	5.5	8	5.4	14	5.5
Speech impediment (stammering, stuttering, lisping)	4	3.7	7	4.7	11	4.3
Conflict with members of family	7	6.4	31	20.9	38	14.8
Rebelliousness	5	4.6	63	42.5	68	26.5
Attention seeking	2	1.8	10	6.8	12	4.7
Sneakiness	7	6.4	21	14.2	28	10.9
Destructiveness	1	0.9	15	10.1	16	6.3
Brazenness	11	10.2	48	32.4	59	23.0
Habitual lying	2	1.8	16	10.8	18	7.0
Temper tantrums	10	9.2	34	23.0	44	17.2
Total disorders per 100 cases	90	24.3†	280	75.7†		

* More than one disorder listed for some cases.

† Percentages calculated on the basis of the total disorders in the two groups per 100 cases.

yet, when gambling assumes the proportions indicated in Table 10, with a boy so strongly addicted to the excitement and routine that he steals at home or outside in order to indulge the habit, and persists in it against the admonitions of parents and teachers, it is important in the total personality of the boy.

Smoking. As listed in Table 10, this refers to an excessive indulgence in and craving for tobacco, and not to an occasional use of a cigarette to achieve a thrill or gain significance in the eyes of a group. In this category are listed 16 cases of the mixed group, and 5 of the primary. Healy and Bronner[2] find 30 per cent of their delinquents engaging in much smoking.

Alcoholism (and Drug Addiction). It is significant to note that there are 11 cases of alcoholism listed in the mixed group, and not a single instance in the primary group. Alcoholism in a youngster does not connote the severity or continuity of indulgence implied in the case of an adult. Nevertheless, the practice is so damaging to the morals of a juvenile that any indulgence in intoxicants warrants consideration. It often leads to premature sophistication in matters of sex, participation in unsupervised parties, and late hours. There was not a single instance of the use of drugs in either group.

Delinquency Habit. This item denotes a chronic habit of committing various offenses in apparent disregard of the social codes. In this classification we find 26 instances (17.6 per cent) in the mixed group. The absence of this trait in the primary group is to be expected from the original definition (p. 2).

Enuresis (Bed Wetting) and Soiling. Enuresis is a condition often referred to as "weak bladder." Actually, bed wetting is a faulty habit, resulting from lack of proper training during the formative years, or from severe nervousness. Bed wetting varies in severity and frequency, and may occur in one boy only as the result of an exciting experience, while in another child it may be a nightly occurrence. As a rule, however, even the worst bed wetters gain bladder control during early adolescence, and beyond the age of 16 it is a very rare occurrence.[3]

Among the mixed group 23 per cent are bed wetters, and

[2] *Op. cit.*, p. 52.

[3] Wile notes that drugs are not necessary for treatment in the case of 95 per cent of enuretics, since the condition disappears spontaneously: *op. cit.*, p. 28.

in the primary 17.6 per cent. The slightly greater frequency in the mixed group is to be expected from the greater nervousness noted among them (p. 53). Soiling, or lack of control of the rectal sphincter, is a nervous habit that is very rarely found among older children.

Nail Biting. Of itself, this has little significance for the health and welfare of a child, but combined with other neurotic traits it serves to confirm the existence of an unhealthy personality pattern. In the mixed group are found 13.5 per cent with this habit, and in the primary 6.4 per cent.

Face and Head Tics. These are nervously generated mannerisms or habits manifested in frequently recurring, annoying, and disturbing movements of the lips, face, eyes, and head. They occasionally spread to include jerking movements of one shoulder or the other. The habit, once established, is fairly difficult to eradicate. Such affections appear among 4.1 per cent of mixed group cases, and in only one case of the primary group.

Sleep Disorders. Sleep walking and sleep talking are disturbing symptoms in children, and regularly imply a highly nervous type of constitution. In line with previous findings of greater nervousness among mixed group children (pp. 58 and 60), we find *15 per cent* of the mixed group suffering from sleep disorders, as compared with *only 2 per cent* of the primary. *Occasional* sleep talking among children of 4 to 10 years of age, particularly under exciting situations, is a fairly common occurrence, and of no special significance. Regularly recurring sleep talking, however, especially in a child past 10 years of age, is a sign of nervous ill health. Sleep walking is always an unhealthy sign. Sleeping with a mother or sister is unhealthy for a grown boy, and *should be regularly condemned.* Nightmares and fear of the dark are in themselves not significant, except as they reflect nervousness in the individual.

Effeminacy. This condition is usually found among oversheltered children, particularly *only* children who are deprived of active and vigorous participation in play and athletics because of parents' fears that bodily injury might come to their offspring. The condition lends itself readily to correction. The so-called "sissy" type is found evenly distributed in the two groups (5.5 per cent as against 5.4 per cent), and hence this trait cannot be considered as a factor in one group as compared with the other.

Speech Impediments. These disorders are usually functional. Occasionally, lisping (tongue-tie) is due to an organic defect in the tongue, easily corrected by surgery. Speech disturbances appear in 4.7 per cent of the mixed group and in 3.7 per cent of the primary. Speech defects *can* and *should* be remedied in early life.

Conflict with Members of Family. This was found among 20.9 per cent of the mixed group members, as against only 6.4 per cent of the primary group. Conflict may vary in degree, from an open revolt against all parental authority and control, to the limited tension occasioned by rivalry with a sibling.

Rebelliousness. This is found among 43.5 per cent of the mixed group cases, as against only 4.6 per cent of the primary group. The large incidence of rebellion against authority, control, and direction among mixed group members bears a probable strong relationship to the almost universal maladjustment found among them (late hours, gang life, maladjustment at school, demoralizing recreation, etc.; see chap. iv).

Attention Seeking. This is found among 6.8 per cent of the mixed group, and 1.8 per cent of the primary. The demand for attention from family, teachers, and others is usually associated with feelings of inadequacy, which, if not properly adjusted and directed, may aggravate other behavior disturbances.

Sneak Behavior. This habit appears among 14.2 per cent of mixed group cases, as compared with 6.4 per cent of the primary group, or with a critical ratio of difference of 3.0, which indicates reliability. This large ratio in the mixed group is rather surprising, since from the comparatively greater timidity of primary group children (see Table 9), one might have expected a much greater incidence of sneakiness among the latter.

Destructiveness. This appears in 15 cases of the mixed group, as against one instance in the primary group. It is probably linked to other phases of disrespect for parental and social authority and the rights and property of others, since the destructive behavior took place within the home as well as at school and in the community.

Brazenness. This manifestation occurred three times as frequently in the mixed group as in the primary (32.4 per cent as against 10.2 per cent). The far greater incidence in the mixed group is probably related to the general aggressiveness of its members (p. 62).

Habitual Lying. This trait appears in greater frequency among the mixed group, with a score of 10.9 per cent, as compared with 1.8 per cent for the primary group. Knowledge of this trait depends in great measure upon information submitted by parents. In the item are also included instances where money is borrowed at local stores for personal use, under pretext that it is intended for the parents, as well as instances where change from shopping errands is appropriated by boys in false accounts to parents, etc. On the subject of lying, Kempf has this to say:

> The grand old law, that "honesty is the best policy," has a critical significance in the development of personal power. It often requires the endurance of great anxiety to honestly endure the prospect of failure, particularly when a dishonest adaptation, as a lie, may give temporary relief or advantage to the cravings and tensions. But the enduring of anxiety in turn gives the individual a sublime reward in that the autonomic apparatus is so constituted that the situation of tension forces it to augment its vigor and thereby develop and acquire skills, endurance, insight, and power in honest competition with his milieu, for the recognized adaptation of just autonomic demands.[4]

[4] *Op. cit.*, p. 59.

Temper Tantrums. Tantrums are overt exhibitionisms, intended to compensate for deeper-lying states of cowardliness and inadequacy, as when motivated to gain undeserved attention, favors, or satisfactions, especially from the mother. They appear most commonly in overindulged and spoiled children. The condition can readily be corrected during early life, but is difficult to remedy once the pattern becomes strongly fixed. It is found to occur in 23 per cent of the mixed group as against 9.2 per cent of the primary group, or with a critical ratio of difference of 3.1.

SUMMARY

Among temperament disorders (Table 9) are listed 227 instances per 100 cases for the mixed group, as compared with 74 instances per 100 cases for the primary group. The high reliability of differences in temperament between the two groups is reflected in the critical ratio of 8.3.

Very significant also is the finding that the most disturbing temperament disorders of surliness, callousness, cruelty, restlessness, stubbornness, and aggressiveness appear six to ten times as often among the mixed group members as among the primary. This indicates that sharp differences in personality separate the mixed group boy from the primary, and these are probably responsible for the marked differences in behavior between the two groups, and are likely to operate as major factors in the outcomes.

Among behavior abnormalities listed in Table 10 appear a total of 280 instances per 100 cases of the mixed group, as compared with 90 for the primary group, or a ratio of 75.7 per cent to 24.3 per cent. The critical ratio of the difference is 8.4, indicating high reliability. Furthermore, the conduct disorders of rebelliousness, gambling, alcoholism, conflict with family, destructiveness, sneakiness, temper tantrums, and habitual lying occur in a frequency four to fifteen times as great in the mixed group as in the primary. The listed behavior abnormalities, together with school maladjustment,

Chapter VIII

TYPES OF JUVENILE OFFENSES

SEX OFFENSES

THE VARIOUS types of juvenile sex offenses will be considered individually, together with frequencies in the two groups, findings as to the nature and significance of certain types of sex offenses, and comments from the literature where indicated. The more serious and aggressive sex acts, such as forceful sex attempts with little girls or women, incest with sisters, sadism, active sodomy, etc., were committed by postpubescents, and the passive and petty acts of perversion by prepubescents. The collected data will appear in the summary.

Excessive Masturbation. Table 11 lists this for 40 instances or 37 per cent of the primary group, and for 40 instances or 27 per cent of the mixed group. The critical ratio of the difference, being only 1.6, lacks reliability. In this item are included instances of mutual masturbation.

Healy and Bronner[1] mention 25 per cent of their delinquents as practicing extreme masturbation, which implies that every fourth case was a serious masturbating problem. These figures serve to reflect the intensity of glandular and emotional excitement among early adolescents, and the great need for proper sex hygiene preparation of juveniles as a protection against still other and worse sex practices, such as appear in Table 11. In this connection, Kempf states:

> The practice of some masturbation is almost universal at this age [adolescence], and is not to be considered harmful if not excessive, and if it does not exclude the seeking of playmates and winning their esteem. The self-loving, fanciful, auto-erotic individual cares little for the world, except to be aggrandized and otherwise left alone to dream and brood.[2]

[1] *Op. cit.*, p. 52.
[2] *Op. cit.*, p. 131.

TABLE 11.—*Types of Juvenile Sex Offenses* Committed by Primary and Mixed Groups*

Type of Sex Offense	Primary Group 108 Cases		Mixed Group 148 Cases		Total 256 Cases	
	No. of Cases	Per-centage	No. of Cases	Per-centage	No. of Cases	Per-centage
Masturbation, excessive	36	33.3	35	23.6	71	27.7
mutual	4	3.7	5	3.4	9	3.5
Self-exposure (exhibitionism)	10	9.2	15	10.1	25	9.8
Peeping	5	4.6	4	2.7	9	3.5
Pronounced obscenity (spoken or written)	7	6.4	40	27.0	47	18.4
Fellatio, active	9	8.3	16	10.8	25	9.8
passive	10	9.2	12	8.1	22	8.6
Sodomy, with father or older siblings	4	3.7	10	6.8	14	5.5
with other adult	18	16.6	32	21.6	50	19.5
with boy of equal age	13	12.0	13	8.8	26	10.2
with younger boy	5	4.6	2	1.3	7	2.7
with girl	3	2.8	4	2.7	7	2.7
with younger siblings	4	3.7	0	0.1	4	1.6
All types of perversion	7	6.4	16	10.8	23	9.0
Group affairs with girls	3	2.8	0	0.0	3	1.2
Sex attempt with little girl	8	7.2	17	11.5	25	9.8
Heterosexual experiences	12	11.1	11	7.4	23	9.0
Touching little girls' parts	11	10.2	15	10.1	26	10.2
sisters' parts	2	1.8	3	2.0	5	2.0
woman's parts	5	4.6	13	2.0	18	3.1
Incest with sisters	1	0.9	12†	8.1	13	5.1
attempted with mother	1	0.9	0	0.0	1	0.4
Sadism	3	2.8	4	2.7	7	2.7
Violent sex assault on woman	0	0.0	1	0.7	1	0.4
Total sex offenses per 100 cases	168	48.0‡	182	52.0‡		
Average (M) of sex offenses per case	1.7		1.8			

* More than one offense listed for some of the cases.

† Two of the sisters became pregnant and gave birth.

‡ Percentages are calculated on the basis of total offenses in each group per 100 cases.

And again, Kempf writes:

At this transition [into adolescence], boys and girls tend to become serious rivals for overt demonstrations of the esteem of the members of the opposite sex, particularly of their own age.   This necessitates courageous competition, steadiness and self-control in trials, and a willingness to suffer from defeats, as well as to enjoy the glories of victory—heroic age of athletes, and self-conquest, and writings and reading of romantic literature.[3]

That this idea is not entirely new, may be shown from the following quotation from Rousseau's *Emile*:

My son, there is no happiness without courage, nor virtue without struggle—by virtue is meant strength of will—this need arises with the awakening of the passions.[4]

Zachry states:

With this increased tension in his growing sexual maturity [adolescence] he is beginning to see some things that before would have passed unnoticed and to see accustomed things in a new light.   He is engrossed in love and adventure stories, motion pictures, newspapers, new dances, and swing bands.[5]

Havelock Ellis reveals the following:

Of 347 academic students, 71 denied that they practiced masturbation, which seems to imply that 79 per cent admitted that they practiced it.[6]

Hitschman states:

Masturbation in the littlest children seldom and only in excessive cases demands the interference of the parent or tutor—onanism [at 3 to 5 years] must within some limits be considered a normal phenomenon.   This is normally soon replaced by the so-called latent period, when all sex is dormant.   If the practice during this prepuberty period is excessive it must be checked, but not by gruff and terrifying prohibition.   The masturbation of puberty cannot be entirely

[3] *Op. cit.*, p. 135.
[4] *Op. cit.*, p. 408.
[5] Zachry, C. B., *Emotion and Conduct in Adolescence*, p. 45.
[6] Ellis, H., *Studies in the Psychopathology of Sex*, vol. 6, p. 236.

avoided, because in our civilized social organization too great an interval has been interposed between the awakening of the sex instinct and the possibility of its gratification.[7]

Excessive masturbation should be prevented by redirection of the glandular and visceral energies into channels of vigorous muscular activity, by sports, competitive games, and athletics, as well as wholesome mental preoccupation with an abundance of social interaction. Excessive masturbation finds its most helpless, wretched, and ready victims among the early adolescents of the moody, daydreaming, introspective, and introverted type, who spend too much time in idle or romantic speculation, and too little time in play, exercise, and healthy laughter.

Exhibitionism. Self-exposure occurs with almost equal frequency in the two groups—in 9.2 per cent of primary and 10.1 per cent of mixed group cases—usually appearing among adolescents of the timid, sneaky type. These offenders are almost invariably apprehended in their acts. Zachry states:

It is significant in this connection that the boy gave evidence also of conflict directly related to his sexuality. He had formed the habit of wandering about the upstairs rooms of his home from time to time without his clothes, as a very young child might do.[8]

Peeping. This was found in 4.6 per cent of the primary group cases and 2.7 per cent of the mixed group (individuals who seek to derive erotic satisfaction from peeping are often referred to as "voyeurs"). The same personality type operates here as in exhibitionism, but these offenders are not as regularly apprehended. One adolescent is reported to have hammered a small hole through the roof of a women's lavatory in a subway station.

Obscenity. This concerns the use of vulgar language in written or spoken form, the sending of lewd messages to teach-

[7] Hitschman, E. H., *Freud's Theories of the Neuroses*, p. 20.
[8] *Op. cit.*, p. 108.

ers or girls, etc. It was found among 6.4 per cent of primary and 27 per cent of mixed group cases. This rather large difference in the two groups, equal to a critical ratio of 4.8, bears probable relations to the more disorganized and generally aggressive behavior of members of the mixed group.

On the subject of salacious literature, Carr states:

A Los Angeles police officer in 1939 placed the number of magazines glorifying crime or exploiting sex in the United States at 421. A check list used by a reform agency of that city specifically named 73, most of which had recently published material violating state obscenity laws.[9]

Fellatio. Perversion by mouth, both active and passive, was found in a total of 19 instances of the primary group, or 17.5 per cent, as against 28 cases, or 18.9 per cent, of the mixed group. The passive form is found chiefly among prepubescent, defenseless children who are forced or bribed into the act, while the active form appears predominantly among the adolescents.

Sodomy. Perversion by the anus with adults, small boys, young girls, or with the father or older siblings, occurred in a total of 47 instances, or 43.4 per cent, of the primary group, and in 61 instances, or 41.2 per cent, of the mixed group. Vulgarisms frequently applied to the practice are "buggery" and "goosing." The different types and frequencies of sodomy appear in Table 11. The adolescent seeks in this activity a physical substitute for distasteful masturbation and a mental substitute for sexual intercourse. The remarkably uniform distribution of this and the preceding item among cases in the two groups deserves particular notice.

It should be realized that perversions of this type occur much more commonly among juveniles than is surmised, and find their counterpart in some of the tribal rituals of our present day, according to Westermarck: "Sodomistic acts are committed with the sacred men of a tribe. . . . In Morocco,

[9] Carr, L. J., *Delinquency Control*, p. 229.

supernatural benefits are to this day expected to derive not only from heterosexual but also from homosexual intercourse with a holy person."[10]

All Types of Perversion. This condition was found among 7 cases, or 6.4 per cent, of the primary group, and in 16 cases, or 10.8 per cent, of the mixed sex group. Under this classification are included boys that had engaged in all varieties of perversion, sodomy, fellatio, mutual masturbation, etc., usually in passive roles, as weak or immature individuals, or under pressure or bribe.

Group Affairs with Girls. These occurred in only 3 cases of the primary group, and in none of the mixed group. They were of the mild petting and inspecting nature, and occurred in a group of children on a roof adjoining a school.

Sex Attempt with Little Girls. This appeared in 8 instances of the primary group, or 7.4 per cent, and 17 instances, or 11.5 per cent, of the mixed group. The critical ratio of the difference, being only 1.1, shows an absence of reliability. These events consisted chiefly of surface attempts at gratification on the bodies of the little girls, but in a few instances there was actual attempt at penetration, with physical and emotional injury to the girl.

Heterosexual Experiences. These include instances of sexual intercourse with adolescent girls and women and occurred in 12 cases of the primary group, or 11.1 per cent, and in 11 cases, or 7.4 per cent, of the mixed group. Rousseau (who from his own life's experience must have known) declares, in his classic treatise *Emile*, that "his horror of adultery and debauch keeps him at a distance from prostitutes and married women, and the disorders of youth may always be traced to one or the other."[11]

Blos states: "Only through wayward conduct, such as truancy and tramping, or through overt sex relationships,

[10] Westermarck, E., *The History of Human Marriage*, vol. 1, p. 224.
[11] *Op. cit.*, p. 296.

could he convince himself that he possessed the self-determination, independence, and mature masculinity which he so markedly lacked."[12]

Touching or Exploring Sisters', Women's, or Little Girls' Parts. This occurred among 18, or 16.6 per cent, of the primary group cases, and in 21, or 14.1 per cent, of the mixed group cases. Inspection of a sister's sex parts occurs much more commonly than is revealed in Table 11, and is usually of no serious import to the life of either child, if otherwise well balanced, although parents learning of the events may become greatly perturbed. The same applies to instances of touching and inspecting little girls. Cases, however, where a strongly charged erotic impulse leads an adolescent to touch forcibly the body of an adult woman, are of a far more serious nature, the experience very often involving a severe physical and emotional shock to the woman, who, in the excitement, is not infrequently thrown to the ground by the adolescent.

Incest with Sister. This was found to exist in one case, or 0.9 per cent, of the primary group, as against 12 such instances, or 8.1 per cent, of the mixed group cases. The critical ratio of the difference is 3.3, which signifies reliability. These sex situations were very morbid, and two of the sisters in the mixed group became pregnant and gave birth to babies, as a result of the incest. Parents or guardians were regularly found to have contributed to these unfortunate happenings through lack of proper supervision and guidance of their offspring.

Incest Attempt with Mother. This occurred in only one instance in the primary group and was found upon actual study not to have involved the specific aim of intercourse, but rather a crazed and excited adolescent urge to grasp the widowed mother's breasts, and to touch her naked body. The excitation was contributed to in part by the mother's wearing of thin loose garments during the heat of the summer. In the

[12] Blos, P., *The Adolescent Personality*, p. 474.

process of grabbing at his mother the boy tore her dress, which quickly brought him to his senses, in a rather severely shocked state of mind; later on probation the boy responded well.

A remark by Kempf applies in any husbandless situation:

> The mother who obtains a separation or divorce sometimes encourages the son to feel that he is his mother's hero. He enthusiastically responds with affection for her and prematurely seeks responsibility. This affection, as he matures, if not effectively sublimated, will be likely to express itself frankly, at first, in dreams, and then in obsessive cravings, in the form of sexual interest in the mother.[13]

Sadism. This occurred in 3 instances, or 2.8 per cent, of the primary group, and in 4 instances, or 2.7 per cent, of the mixed group. One instance concerned an adolescent who scarred a little boy's sex organ with a burning stick, deriving morbid gratification from the suffering of the child. The others were cases of marked brutality toward girls, without any actual sexual attempt. Sadism in a boy does not connote severity nor regularity of practice as when the term is applied to an adult. On sadism as a substitute for the sex act, Pfister offers the following instances:

> A 14-year-boy hates his younger brother and torments him—every morning he awakes him by sticking his finger into his mouth—the patient had been misused pederastically by associates, erotically excited, and tried the act symbolically on his brother with the finger.[14]
>
> A 16-year-year-old boy saw a cat sitting in the sun; unrest seized him; he procured a stick and struck the sleeping cat on the nose full force; the young cat was half dead with pain and fright, but the boy had a morbid sense of pleasure, in torture he felt the sweetest delight and sexual orgasm.[15]

Violent Sex Assault on a Woman. This occurred in only one instance, that of a 15-year-old mixed group adolescent who,

[13] *Op. cit.*, p. 99.
[14] Pfister, *op. cit.*, p. 158.
[15] *Ibid.*, p. 77.

in a violent fit of sex madness, brutally assaulted and almost killed the wife of a tenant in his father's house, during the absence of the woman's husband. This boy later displayed evidence of an undefined mental derangement, was repeatedly brought before adult courts for assault, robbery, and arson, and is now confined in Sing Sing prison (see case A.C., p. 113).

There may have been other instances of sex offenses committed by members of the two groups that remain unknown or undisclosed, and hence unlisted in Table 11; but the data submitted provide adequate insight into the most common

TABLE 12.—*Type of Role Assumed by Delinquents in Sex Offenses**

Type of Role	Primary Group 108 Cases		Mixed Group 148 Cases		Total 256 Cases	
	No. of Cases	Percentage	No. of Cases	Percentage	No. of Cases	Percentage
Passive	33	30.5	34	23.0	67	26.1
Wilful	41	38.0	59	39.8	100	39.0
Forcible	28	25.9	41	27.7	69	27.0
Violent	3	2.8	13	8.8	16	6.3
Undetermined	3	2.8	1	0.7	4	1.6
Total	108	100.0	148	100.0	256	

* Chief role only shown for each offender.

types of sex offense committed by pre- and post-adolescent boys in the community, in the home, and in institutions.

It is of interest to note, in Table 11, that there were 168 sex offenses per 100 primary cases, and 182 such offenses per 100 mixed group cases, or a critical ratio of difference of 0.5, which is insignificant.

ROLE IN SEX DELINQUENCY

The roles assumed during the sex offense by members of the two groups appear in Table 12.

The roles played in the sex acts show no major variations in the two groups, as classified in Table 12, indicating that neither the sex role nor the type of sex offense (see Table 11) constitutes a proper basis for judging or treating a sex offender. Almost all the forcible and violent sex acts were performed by postpubescents, while the prepubescents engaged largely in minor and passive sex roles.

CAUSES OF SEX DELINQUENCY

As stated on page 3, our investigation is primarily concerned with discovering basic factors in the personality and behavior of the compared sex offenders that stand in relation to success or failure in later life, as criteria for forecast and treatment. Of lesser import to this study are the factors that contribute to or cause juvenile sex delinquency, which has been shown in this chapter to be fairly similar in the two groups, as regards type, frequency, and role. It is obvious therefore that it is not the nature or causes of juvenile sex offenses that will bear relationship to any differences that may appear in the outcomes of the two groups, but rather the factors in the background, personality, and general behavior of the sex offenders, which have already been shown to be widely diverse in the two groups. Nevertheless, in conformity with original intentions (p. 3), a cursory statement of the contributing and determining causes of juvenile sexual delinquency, as derived from the analyses of the case records, will be offered.

The findings of the study warrant the axiomatic conclusion that no trait, or combination of traits, operates as a specific cause of juvenile sexual delinquency. A variety of causes, of both extrinsic and intrinsic origin, are elicited from the case records.

Most significant among the extrinsic or determining causes are lack of proper guidance in sex hygiene and inadequate protection of children by parents. Others to be listed are: intimidation and seduction of junior members of a gang by their leaders; the urge in young boys to gain the friendship and protection of older members of a gang; imitation of other boys; the lure of money and favors from adult degenerates; pressure threats from depraved adults; curiosity and excitement aroused in pubescents by pornographic literature or lewd talk; the practice of unwisely leaving children to the care of immoral and conniving adolescents or adults; permitting of grown children to sleep together; the leaving of adolescent siblings of opposite sex unsupervised for long periods; degenerate, immoral, or incompetent parents; mothers who impart intimate information about their children to seemingly benign elderly degenerates, etc.

The intrinsic or contributing causes include puberty, effeminacy, physical inadequacy, timidity, endocrine disorders, etc. These serve to predispose to but do not determine or precipitate the sex offenses, except in isolated instances. As noted on page 56, glandular disorders are relatively insignificant. Puberty is the most important of the intrinsic causes, and denotes the stage of life when the sexual glands mature and induce bodily and mental excitation, curiosity, general restlessness, and a temptation toward sexual or substitute-sexual gratification. Puberty thus strongly contributes to the commission of sex offenses, but, without benefit of extrinsic factors, the force of puberty would not of itself eventuate in the commission of the sexually delinquent act. Garrison states that "the sexual drive is greatly augmented near a time of somatic puberty and continues to grow in strength for some time thereafter by virtue of factors of maturation and sexual contacts and experiences."[16]

OFFENSES OTHER THAN SEXUAL

The various types of juvenile general offenses, or offenses other than sexual, appear in Diagram 9 and Table 13, together with the frequencies of these among members of the two compared groups. The listed offenses include desertion of home, chronic truancy, ungovernable and mischievous behavior, peculation, stealing, pyromania, robbery, burglary, and violent assault.

The data on general offenses are not submitted with the purpose of contrasting frequencies in the two groups, since by

[16] *Op. cit.*, p. 91.

original definition (p. 2) the primary cases were accepted as free of any known offenses other than sexual. The data on general offenses are presented rather with the expressed pur-

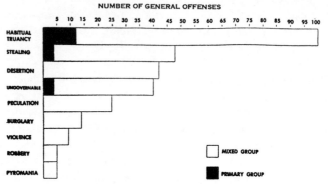

DIAGRAM 9. TYPES OF GENERAL OFFENSES COMMITTED BY JUVENILE SEX DELINQUENTS OF PRIMARY AND OF MIXED GROUP

TABLE 13.—*Juvenile Offenses Other than Sexual*

Type of Offense	Primary Group 108 Cases		Mixed Group 148 Cases		Total 256 Cases	
	No.	Percentage	No.	Percentage	No.	Percentage
Desertion			42	28.4	42	16.8
Chronic truancy	12	11.1	88	59.6	100	39.1
Ungovernableness	4	3.7	36	24.3	40	16.1
Peculation	3	2.7	25	16.9	28	10.9
Stealing	1	0.9	43	29.0	44	17.2
Pyromania			5	3.4	5	2.0
Robbery			5*	3.4	5	2.0
Burglary			14	9.5	14	5.5
Violence			9	6.1	9	3.5
Total	20		267		287	

* Three of these boys used revolvers, one with open intent to kill.

pose of revealing the serious extent of these offenses among the mixed group members, as outgrowths of the pronounced abnormalities in background and personality noted in chapters II, III, IV, and VII.

The 12 boys of the primary group who were involved in twenty instances of petty general offenses—truancy (12), ungovernableness (4), peculation (3), and pilfering (1)—rightfully belong with the mixed group cases, but the discrepancy came to attention only after the statistical digest of the two groups of cases was on the way to completion. Separate attention will, however, be devoted to these 12 cases in the section on outcomes, and, interestingly enough, they do not thus far seem to have influenced the marked differences in traits disclosed among members of the two compared groups.

Little comment seems warranted as to the number and nature of the individual nonsexual offenses, because, first, the primary concern of the study is sex offenses, and, second, these data are presented merely to illustrate the extent of behavior morbidity among mixed group cases, with 3 of these boys using guns—one with intent to kill. This purpose is fully met by the contents of the table and diagram.

COURT AND CLINIC TREATMENT OF THE OFFENDERS

Clinic Recommendations and Court Dispositions. The court justices are not obliged to accept the recommendations of the court clinics with regard to cases referred by the courts for clinic study. The Gluecks,[17] in a carefully conducted survey, implied that there had been a deplorable lack of conformity between the types of treatment carried out by the justices of the Boston Juvenile Court and the recommendations sub-

[17] The Gluecks comment on court and clinic cooperation (in a study of cases treated by the Boston Juvenile Court and Judge Baker Foundation Guidance Clinic) as follows: "A substantial proportion of the clinic's recommendations were not put into effect by the court (and its agents). Thus, the place-of-living recommendations were not executed at all in one-fifth of the cases; so also two-thirds of those involving placement in a foster home or with relatives were not carried out; and over two-fifths of the recommendations for placement in the country or in a school for the feebleminded were not followed. . . . But it seems to be a legitimate inference that where so high a proportion of the recommendations of the clinic were not followed by the court, or in the relationships of court and clinic to the other agencies, it operated to the disadvantage of the children": *op. cit.*, pp. 128, 132.

mitted by the Boston Court Clinic, which could not but have operated to the disadvantage of the children. In this light, the data in Table 14 and Diagram 10 are highly gratifying, in that they reveal a remarkable regularity of cooperation between

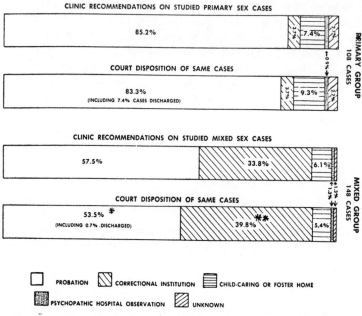

CLINIC RECOMMENDATIONS ON STUDIED PRIMARY SEX CASES

85.2% 3.7% 7.4%

PRIMARY GROUP 108 CASES

COURT DISPOSITION OF SAME CASES

83.3% (INCLUDING 7.4% CASES DISCHARGED) 3.7% 9.3%

CLINIC RECOMMENDATIONS ON STUDIED MIXED SEX CASES

57.5% 33.8% 6.1%

MIXED GROUP 148 CASES

COURT DISPOSITION OF SAME CASES

53.5% * (INCLUDING 0.7% DISCHARGED) 39.8% ** 5.4%

☐ PROBATION   ⧄ CORRECTIONAL INSTITUTION   ☰ CHILD-CARING OR FOSTER HOME
▨ PSYCHOPATHIC HOSPITAL OBSERVATION   ▧ UNKNOWN

* It is not in the province of the clinic but of the court to recommend discharge on an offense.
** In addition, 10.1 per cent of the probation cases failed and were sent to correctional institutions.

DIAGRAM 10. CLINIC RECOMMENDATIONS AND COURT DISPOSITIONS IN 256 CASES OF JUVENILE SEX DELINQUENCY OF PRIMARY AND OF MIXED GROUP, 1928–1934

the justices and the clinics of the juvenile courts in New York City. This is all the more surprising since the cases utilized in the investigation cover a six-year period, during which they were under the care and study of many doctors and justices of the juvenile courts, in five different boroughs of New York City.

As the largest difference between the treatment plans of the clinics and judges shows a critical ratio of only 1.0, which is insignificant, it is apparent that a spirit of agreement motivated these two agencies of the children's courts, which should have

TABLE 14.—*Clinic Recommendations and Court Dispositions in Cases of Primary and Mixed Group Delinquents*

Group		Clinic Recommendations†					Court Dispositions					
		Probation	Remand or Commitment to Correctional Institution	To Child Care Institutions and Foster Placement	Remand to Psychopathic Hospital	Total	Probation	Remanded or Committed to Correctional Institution	To Child Care Institutions and Foster Placement	Remanded to Psychopathic Hsopital	Discharged	Total
Primary 108 cases	no. of cases	92	4	8	1	105*	82	4	10	1	8	105*
	percentage	85.2	3.7	7.4	0.9	97.2	75.9	3.7	9.2	0.9	7.4	97.2
Mixed 148 cases	no. of cases	85	50	9	2	146*	78	59‡	8	2	1	146*
	percentage	57.5	33.8	6.1	1.3	98.6	52.8	39.8	5.4	1.3	0.7	98.6
Total 256 cases	no. of cases	177	54	17	3	251	160	63‡	18	3	9	251
	percentage	69.1	21.1	6.7	1.2	98.0	62.5	24.6	7.0	1.2	3.5	98

* Three cases returned to their native states, from which they had deserted; 2 mixed group cases transferred to Court of Special Sessions because of overage status.

† It is not within the scope of the clinic to make recommendations for discharge, hence no corresponding column appears for clinic recommendations.

‡ Plus 15 who failed probation.

worked to the benefit of the children. The following tabulation brings this into clear perspective:

	Primary Group Percentage		Mixed Group Percentage	
	Probation	Commitment	Probation	Commitment
Clinic recommendations	85.2	3.7	57.5	33.8
Court dispositions	83.3	3.7	53.5	39.8

REVISITS TO COURT CLINICS

The data in Table 15 reveal that a total of 682 revisits were made by the delinquents in the two groups who were on probation, with an average (M) of 3 visits for the primary group and 2.5 for the mixed group.   The table also reveals a total of 651 months of court clinic supervision for the 132 cases of both groups on probation, or an average (M) of 5.5 months for the primary group, and 4.3 months for the mixed.   The modal

TABLE 15.—*Number of Visits to and Months of Supervision by Court Clinics*

No. Visits	Primary 108 Cases		Mixed 148 Cases		Total 256 Cases		No. Months Supervision	Primary 108 Cases		Mixed 148 Cases		Total 256 Cases	
	No. of Cases	Per-cent-age	No. of Cases	Per-cent-age	No. of Cases	Per-cent-age		No. of Cases	Per-cent-age	No. of Cases	Per-cent-age	No. of Cases	Per-cent-age
1	42	38.8	82	55.5	124	48.4	1	2	1.8	5	3.4	7	2.7
2	14	12.9	18	12.2	32	12.5	2	3	2.8	14	9.5	17	6.7
3	17	15.7	15	10.1	32	12.5	3	8	7.4	11	7.4	19	7.4
4	10	9.2	11	7.4	21	8.2	4	3	2.8	9	6.1	12	4.7
5	14	12.9	7	4.7	21	8.2	5	12	11.1	8	5.4	20	7.8
6	4	3.7	2	1.3	6	2.3	6	21	19.4	5	3.4	26	10.2
7	3	2.8	4	2.7	7	2.7	7	9	8.3	5	3.4	14	5.5
8	2	1.8	2	1.3	4	1.6	8	4	3.7	3	2.0	7	2.7
9	0	0.0	1	0.7	1	0.4	9	1	0.9	0	0.0	1	0.4
10+	2	1.8	6	4.1	8	3.1	10+	3	2.8	6	4.1	9	3.5
Total	108	100.0	148	100.0	256	100.0	Total	66*	60.0	66*	44.7	132	51.6

* This figure represents total number continuing under clinic supervision, since 42 primary group cases, and 82 mixed group cases, had only an original examination.

concentration in the mixed group is at 2 months, whereas in the primary group it is at 6 months, indicating greater cooperation for clinic treatment among the latter.

SUMMARY

Table 11 shows a total of 168 sex offenses per 100 cases of the primary group, and 182 per 100 of the mixed group.   The critical ratio of the difference is 0.5, which is insignificant.

In considering the types of sex offenses, the only item signally different in the two compared groups is the occurrence of twelve instances of incest with sisters in the mixed group; two of these girls became pregnant and bore babies, a rather sordid index of the extent of disorganization in the homes of these delinquents. There was only one instance of attempted incest in the primary group.

Other than this, the primary group boys engaged in as many and in the same kind of sex offenses as the mixed group boys (Table 11), and with fairly equal forcibleness, wilfulness, and violence (Table 12). It should therefore be apparent that, if the prediction for and treatment of a sex delinquent were to rest *entirely on the type and severity of his sex offense*, great injustice might be done to boys with good prospects, and unconstructive leniency possibly shown those with warped minds and poor outlook. The study clearly reveals the need for and importance of *judging the total personality of the child, rather than his sex act*. The wilful, forcible, and violent sex acts are regularly committed by postpubescents, whereas the prepubescents engage in passive sex roles.

The sex offense of greatest frequency listed in Table 11 involves sodomy with fathers, older siblings, other adults, boys of equal age, younger boys, with girls, and with younger siblings, occurring among 43.4 per cent of the primary and 41.2 per cent of the mixed group. While these practices are decidedly unhealthy, and should be condemned, they ought not, when occurring among juveniles, be regarded in too morbid a light, nor should the boys be considered "perverts" or "homosexuals," as noted in some of the texts. The vast majority of offenders engage once or a few times in these unwholesome affairs and turn from them spontaneously with disgust, shame, or fear of exposure. It should be noted, furthermore, that, of the entire series of 256 cases, only two members of the mixed group revealed such deep interest in and craving for homosexual practices as to warrant the designation of "homosexual."

Almost all of the primary group cases, and many of the

mixed group cases, were motivated toward perverted practices (i.e., sodomy, fellatio, mutual masturbation, etc.) by momentary impulse, imitation of others, seduction, force, bribery, curiosity, desire to gain the favor of older members of a gang, or glandular excitement. On sober reflection, almost all the sex delinquents during interviews felt ashamed and guilty of their acts, manifested revulsion toward their experiences, and appeared to retain no trace of inclination toward a return to the practices. It was often interesting to observe hardened delinquents—who displayed no hesitancy in justifying violent acts of assault, stealing, or burglary, on one pretext or another —register deep shame, embarrassment, and guilt over a comparatively minor sex indiscretion. It is inspiring to note that in not a single instance did a boy seek to justify a sex offense.

Offenses other than sexual, or general offenses, occurred in 267 instances in the mixed group, many of them of violent nature, including use of a gun, assault, burglary, robbery, thievery, and pyromania. No detailed treatment is accorded the data, first, because the investigation is primarily concerned with the problem of sex offenses, and, second, because all mixed group boys are by definition general delinquents, on which basis they were originally segregated from the primary group. The nonsexual or general offenses are presented merely to reveal the extent of the morbidity operative among mixed group members, for its significance in regard to the later outcomes. Twelve primary group boys, who were so classified through error, rightfully belong with the mixed group, because they committed twenty petty general offenses (see Table 13). These will receive proper attention in the discussion of outcomes. Thus far, they do not seem to have impaired the significance of the values derived from the analyses of traits in the two compared groups.

A highly gratifying finding of the study was the evidence disclosed in Table 14 of the remarkable uniformity between clinic recommendations and court dispositions operating in the children's courts of New York City. The data in Table 15 reveal that primary probationers report to the clinics more often, and for a longer period of guidance, than do mixed group probationers, suggesting that the former are more receptive to follow-up treatment and redirection.

This concludes the part of the investigation concerned with analyses of traits and factors in personality and behavior of the two compared groups of sex delinquents, as outgrowths of the background conditioning forces, which received attention in preceding sections. The succeeding section will be devoted to analysis and evaluation of the later life behavior of the two compared groups. The last part of the study will seek to provide answers to the original problems motivating the study, and, in addition, will offer a general summation of values and conclusions derived from the study, bearing upon prediction in, prevention, and treatment of juvenile sex delinquency.

PART III

THE OUTCOMES

As originally stated (p. 12), the later life outcomes in this study are to be treated as failures or successes solely according to the criterion of the presence or absence of a verified adult criminal court record of law violations, sexual or general. Traffic or peddling violations are excluded. It is also not feasible, within the province of this investigation, to utilize elements such as idleness, late hours, gambling, disrespect to parents, and happiness or unhappiness in adult life as criteria of success or failure, without passing into the realm of speculation, controversial opinion, and subjective judgment (p. 11). These items will therefore be excluded from the workable data of the analyses but will receive consideration in the interpretations (Part IV). Since the study is primarily concerned with the problem of sex offenses, the sexual failures are to receive first consideration.

It is realized that still other instances of failure besides those to be described may have occurred among the later life events of the juvenile sex offenders, by way of violations in which they were possibly not apprehended, or, if the cases were recorded under aliases, or in distant states, they have not been possible to trace for the study. One limitation—and others will appear in the chapter on conclusions—is that no fingerprint records are available for juveniles, which would aid in tracing the later life careers; hence some known criminals among them may have been missed. However, the search for criminal later life data was so closely checked and cross checked with criminal identification bureaus, courts, probation departments, penal institutions, and public and private agencies,[1]

[1] Acknowledgment is here made of the valuable assistance rendered the investigation by many public and private agencies that gave generously of their

that it is believed that few recorded offenders have been overlooked.[2] Furthermore, the limitations, which are irremediable under present conditions, do not appear to disturb in the least the important findings derived from analyses of the verified failures in the two groups, as will be noted in the succeeding chapters.

The full case histories of all the adult sex failures, together with analyses of their violations, will appear in chapter IX; the adult general failures, with illustrative case history reports, will receive attention in chapter X; a summary of all failures, sexual and general, will appear in chapter XI; and the adult successes, both those of continuous character and those marked with juvenile recidivism, illustrated by typical cases, will appear in chapter XII.

---

time and labor, without which this report would have been impossible. Prominent among these are the following:

Social Service Exchange Clearance Bureau of New York City
Bureau of Criminal Identification, Police Department, New York City
Bureau of Criminal Identification, State of New York
Probation Department, Court of General Sessions, New York City
Probation Department, Kings County Court, Brooklyn, N. Y.
Probation departments, children's courts, New York City
Magistrates courts, New York City
New York State Training School for Boys, Warwick, N. Y.
Children's Village, Dobbs Ferry, N. Y.
Juvenile Aid Bureau, Police Department, New York City
Catholic Guardian Society, New York City

[2] The intimate careers of 4 primary and 10 mixed group juveniles were not possible to establish, 2 having migrated to California; 1 is believed to have died of tuberculosis; 2 were known recidivists after the original offense, but their later behavior remains unknown; and several boys were placed with relatives in distant states. No evidence being available of any violations among the 14 unknown cases, they will arbitrarily have to be counted among the successes, since the original criterion (see p. 12) defines failures as cases with established criminal court records. However, since they represent no more than 5.5 per cent of the series of cases, they could not, even if there had been some failures among them, materially affect the striking trends indicated in the outcomes of the two compared groups (see Diagram 11).

Chapter IX

ADULT SEXUAL FAILURES

THE ADULT failures on the score of sexual violations will receive attention in this chapter. They appear as follows in numerical tabulation:

	Primary Group 108 Cases		Mixed Group 148 Cases		Total 256 Cases	
	No. of Cases	Percentage	No. of Cases	Percentage	No. of Cases	Percentage
Sex failures	0	0	8	5.4	8	3.1
Sex violations	0	0	10	6.8	10	3.9

The absence of adult sexual failures among the primary group members does not warrant a hasty conclusion that a primary group juvenile sex offender never commits a sex offense in later life. It merely indicates that no such instances were found among the members of this group. When, however, consideration is given to the original purpose in segregating the primary group—to represent true juvenile sex offenders as distinguished from the general delinquents of the mixed group (p. 2)—the later life findings are signally important, and should prove helpful to those concerned with problems of treatment and forecast for the true juvenile sex offender.

The members of the mixed group, in contrast to those of the primary group, were not specific sex offenders, but were known to have been involved in various other offenses besides sexual depredations in their juvenile careers; hence their adult sex violations cannot be considered in direct relationship to their juvenile sex offenses. Nevertheless, it should prove instructive to examine the ten violations, among eight mixed group failures (one having committed three such offenses), in itemized form:

Type of Sexual Violation	Number
Sex attempt with young girl*	5†
Stripping and inspecting a little girl	1
Self-exposure to young girls	1
Sodomy with small boys	1
Sodomy with younger sister	1
Accepted perversions with adults	1

* In one instance with a sister.
† One adult killed himself when apprehended in the act.

From the tabulation, it is evident that homosexuality is not a feature in the later life of court-treated juvenile sex offenders, only one known instance of this kind having occurred among the 256 cases in the two groups. Henry[1] refers to such individuals as sex variants, and defines a sex variant as one who has failed to achieve and maintain adult heterosexual modes of sexual expression and has resorted to other modes.

There is a definite shift in the sex objective among the adults. Thus, among the juveniles (see Table 11), more than half of the sexual offenses were with individuals of the same sex, whereas four-fifths of the sexual offenses of the mixed group adults were with individuals of the opposite sex.

The infantile tendencies of peeping and self-exposure, which accounted for nine and twenty-five offenses, respectively, in the juvenile stage, still appear among these young adults, with one instance of each type. The inversion of sex interest to members of the immediate family also continues into adulthood, appearing in two violations.

It is important to note that against a total of 451 sex violations among the juveniles of the two groups, only ten known sex violations appear among mixed group adults (and there probably were very few, if any, unreported offenses, since the conditions for which juvenile sex offenders are often excused from appearing in court [p. 5], no longer operate in adult life).

[1] *Op. cit.*, p. 1023.

CASE HISTORIES

The case histories of all the mixed group sex failures are presented with the thought of shedding further light on the character of these individuals.

Case H. G.   This was a white boy, reared in the Catholic faith, 14 years old at the time of a Children's Court clinic study in December, 1932.   His father was Jewish, a criminal who led an immoral existence, suffered from syphilis, was cruel to his family, and deserted the home five years before this time.   He had several illegal marital ventures; he died in the observation ward of Dannemora Prison, where he had been committed for the holdup and killing of a chauffeur.   The mother was Catholic, a British West Indian, who had lived four years with a Portuguese paramour.   This man, an unskilled laborer, earned $17 a week; the mother confined herself to household duties. The boy bitterly resented the paramour's presence in the home.   The neighborhood was a congested, gang-infested section of the Bronx, New York City.

Harold was the older of two siblings, in the fifth grade at school, where he was poorly adjusted, and a habitual truant.   He was aggressive, excitable, rebellious, stubborn, and something of a bully.   He was brought to the Children's Court in May, 1932, for desertion and stealing, and was placed on probation.   He violated his probation, and in November, 1932, reappeared in the Children's Court for breaking windows at school.   Probation was continued.

In December, 1932, he again appeared in the Children's Court for forceful sex manipulation of a little girl in the school yard.   Clinic study revealed an I.Q. of 78, a mental age of 10 years, 10 months. The diagnosis was psychopathic personality, with convulsive seizures. He was placed on probation.   He continued to behave poorly, deserted his home, peculated, and stole outside in the company of a gang.   He exposed himself sexually to girls at school, and made a sexual assault on a little girl on the roof of a house.   He was also charged with having burned the face of a young girl by viciously throwing a lighted match at her.   For his violations of probation he was remanded to the Catholic Protectory in January, 1933.   During this time and after, he visited the clinic on several occasions, over a period of seventeen months.   He finally seemed slightly improved in attitude and behavior and was discharged from probation in the early part of 1935.

In June, 1935, at the age of 17, he was arrested for third degree burglary and sentenced in the Bronx Court to serve an indeterminate sentence at the Elmira Reformatory. He was paroled in August, 1937. He married, had a son, and was maintained on home relief.

In April, 1939, he met sudden death by jumping from a roof where he was apprehended by some men while engaged in a sexual attempt on a young girl.

It is significant to note that his younger brother, Joseph, had appeared on three successive occasions in the Children's Court for burglaries, was boastful of his antisocial skills and offenses, and had been at the Lincolndale School of the Catholic Protectory in 1936, and the state training school at Warwick in 1938; his cooperation was poor, and his outlook morbid. His later career is unknown.

Case S. B. This boy was white, Jewish, born in New York City, and aged 14 years and 6 months at the time of his Children's Court appearance in June, 1930. His parents were American citizens of Russian birth. The father was a baker earning $35 per week; the mother confined her duties to the home, which was located in a congested residential section of Brooklyn. The children received a fair amount of supervision from the parents.

Simon was the youngest of five children. He was in the second term of high school, a habitual truant, and a problem in the class. He associated with and was dominated by an undesirable group of companions, and showed a strong leaning toward exciting and destructive behavior. His mind was abnormally absorbed with motion pictures. He became very aggressive through the continual influence of street contacts, and manifested considerable restlessness. He was rebellious to parental and school control, sullen, and unstable. He revealed signs of marked nervousness, talked in his sleep, and had a strong nail-biting habit. In November, 1926, he was brought into the Children's Court for stealing at school, and was placed on probation.

In June, 1927, he was reported annoying several girls in the neighborhood and attempting sex intimacies with a 7-year-old girl, through a bribe of 25 cents. He was also apprehended robbing a store in his neighborhood, in the company of friends. He was beyond the control of his parents, and the Children's Court committed him to the Hawthorne School of the Jewish Board of Guardians, where he remained for a period of two and a half years.

Shortly after being returned home, he again became involved in stealing from neighborhood stores, and in making sexual advances to girls. He was returned to the Children's Court clinic and the diagnosis was that of neurotic personality. His I.Q. was found to be 101, and his mental age 14 years, 8 months. He was recommitted by the court to the Hawthorne School of the Jewish Board of Guardians, where he remained this time for a period of three years. He reached the seventh term in high school while there.

In January, 1934, shortly after returning from the institution, he was arrested for impairing the morals of a little girl. He appeared in Special Sessions Court, Brooklyn, and was committed to the House of Refuge, where he remained seventeen months. He was then returned to the home of his parents, where conditions were fairly wholesome and comfortable. All the other siblings bore a good reputation, and the parents were industrious and respected members of the community. Simon held odd jobs in amusement places, and at one time worked on a truck. He was single. For a short time he was an apprentice in the upholstery trade, through the influence of his family.

In April, 1936, a year after his release from the House of Refuge, he was arrested for burglary. He was convicted of the charge and committed to Sing Sing Prison for from one to ten years. From Sing Sing he was transferred to Auburn Prison, and paroled in 1938 to live with his parents once again. He has come into no known criminal behavior since he has been at home, although it is recorded that he contracted venereal disease on two occasions, once since he left prison.

Case G. T. This was a white Catholic boy, 11 years and 7 months old at the time of his original Children's Court appearance in April, 1933. He was born in New York City. His father was a Brazilian and a citizen, his mother an American. The parents were divorced. The mother remarried and her whereabouts remained unknown. The boy continued to live with his father, who earned $30 a week and maintained a comfortable home. The neighborhood, however, was a congested, gang-ridden section of Brooklyn, and the boy had little supervision because the father worked out all day,

Gerard was an aggressive, excitable, stubborn, and restless individual. He was highly nervous, suffered from frequent enuresis, nail biting, and temper tantrums. He was sneaky, unreliable, and attention-seeking. He was uncleanly in body and habits. He was reported as imitating his mother in throwing things when in a temper. He was in the fourth term at school, a habitual truant, and did not attend church. He had a strong fancy for movies, which he visited on every possible occasion.

In April, 1933, he was brought to the Children's Court for participating in all types of perversions with an adult as well as several adolescents, in order to obtain money for movies and other pleasures. He was first introduced to these practices through force and pressure, but later began to accept then willingly, and even to solicit them. The clinic diagnosis was neurosis. His I.Q. was 80 and his mental age 8 years, 6 months. He was placed on probation by the court. He violated probation by committing sodomy on small children, and was committed to the Catholic Protectory, from which institution he was paroled in July, 1937. His conduct continued to be poor. He was sullen and uncooperative toward his father. He had no trade interests, and no regular job. He worked occasionally as a helper on a truck, earning a few dollars a week to meet his spending needs.

In May, 1939, he was arrested for committing a sex assault on a young girl, and was committed by the Kings County Court to a correctional institution, where he has remained up to the present.

Case A. G. The subject was a white native Catholic boy, 15 years and 10 months old at the time of the Children's Court clinic study in December, 1929. His father was a citizen, of Italian birth, who had died two years before. His mother, born in the United States, after burying two husbands was caring for her home and nine children, in addition to doing domestic work outside the home. The home was crowded with children and boarders but was located in a fair residential section of Harrison, N. J.

Allen was the youngest of the children. He received little supervision and at an early age acquired a strong taste for street life, excitement, and adventure. He allied himself with delinquent types and participated in various pilfering expeditions. An older sibling had a reformatory record, but it was not known that any influence emanated from him. Allen peculated at home, became a habitual truant, and ran away from home on several occasions. He left school in the seventh grade, at the age of 15. He worked occasionally. He became involved with a vicious group of adults, who conditioned him to all the practices and ceremonials of homosexualism. He soon made fruitless trips to California on wild adventurous schemes of coming into "big" money through homosexual affairs. Even during intervals at home, when unemployed and pressed for money, he would venture into these practices. He came to New York City from his home in New Jersey because his companions had informed him of the great opportunities existing for homosexuals in the "big city."

In December, 1929, he was brought before the Children's Court of New York City, for soliciting and engaging in homosexual practices as a means of livelihood. Clinic study revealed a neurotic personality, with effeminate acquired mannerisms. He was not considered a fixed homosexual, since it was believed that he had prostituted himself for the adventure and profit derived, rather than through any intrinsic drive for pleasure. Furthermore, he had sought and engaged in heterosexual practices, and had recently kept company for several months with a girl with whom he had had long acquaintance. His I.Q. was found to be 91 and his mental age 14 years, 5 months. The court placed him on probation under supervision of the New Jersey authorities.

In June, 1931, he appeared before the Quarter Sessions Court in Newark, N. J., for homosexual practices, and was committed to state prison for three years. He was transferred to a state reformatory in November, 1933, and paroled the following year.

In January, 1935, he was arrested in New York City for petit larceny, and pleaded guilty in General Sessions Court. He was transferred to New Jersey authorities to remain under probationary supervision until 1942.

Case C. S. This lad was 15 years and 4 months old at the time of a Children's Court clinic study in April, 1932. He was a native white Catholic boy, of native parents. His mother was a woman of unusually low morals, an addict to alcoholism, cruel to the children, a periodic deserter of her children and home, and was known to employ foul language in the home. Charles was born in the Bedford Reformatory, where his mother was an inmate at the time. She had been arrested early in her marital life for stealing a diamond ring and was sent to prison. As Charles grew in years, she took him with her on immoral ventures, and often beat his head against the wall, threatening to kill him if he revealed her escapades to his father. Charles was the oldest of four siblings.

In 1927, he was placed in a child care institution because of the mother's neglect, and shortly thereafter she died. The father, a skilled workman earning $40 a week, remarried shortly after and had the boy return to him. The stepmother was kind, but offered Charles little supervision. The home was kept clean and orderly and was located in a fair section of Brooklyn. Charles was a nervous, unstable, and insecure child. He attended church regularly, but was a truant and a problem at school. He was in conflict with the teachers, and was teased by his classmates because of his effeminate ways. The father noted, much to his chagrin, that his son acted like a "sissy," that boys in the street called him a "pansy," and that he played with younger boys and girls, jumping rope and rolling marbles instead of playing ball and other games with boys of his own age. He was fond of house chores, and liked to wash dishes and floors. He was docile, excitable, restless, a nail biter and a bully with small children.

In April, 1932, he was brought to the Children's Court for committing acts of sodomy on his younger siblings, as well as on other children in the neighborhood. He was also said to be acting queerly, masturbating openly in the presence of other children, and constantly employing lewd language. He was examined in the clinic and diagnosed as a case of psychopathic personality, with effeminate and homosexual traits. He was in the sixth grade at school, his I.Q. was 75 and his mental age 11 years, 6 months. He was placed on probation by the court and revisited the clinic on five occasions, without effective change in habits, manners, or attitudes.

In February, 1933, he reappeared in the Children's Court for much the same type of behavior and was committed to the House of Refuge.

In August, 1934, he was arrested for practicing sodomy with a small boy, and his case appeared in the Court of Special Sessions, New York County. His whereabouts and subsequent progress have not been possible to trace. He is perhaps operating under an assumed name.

Case I. R. This was a white Jewish boy, 15 years old at the time of his Children's Court appearance in July, 1928. He was born in New York City, of Russian parents, who were naturalized citizens.

His father was the owner of a small tailor shop, from which he derived average earnings of $40 a week, while the mother attended to the home, which was found on investigation to be clean and comfortably furnished, and situated in a fair though congested section of the Bronx, New York City.

Isidore was the second of four siblings, and had not been a problem prior to puberty, which set in at the age of 12, but thereafter he began to display increasing signs of an unhealthy personality. He became excitable, unreasonable, moody, impulsive, and restless. He began to show defiance and surliness at home, and resorted to temper tantrums when criticized for his failings. He seemed definitely disturbed, and it was discovered by his family that he engaged in excessive masturbation, for which he refused advice. He discontinued playing games of ball, and sought the companionship of younger children, for reasons that will appear later. He spent much time in daydreaming, both at home and at school. Reading and concentration on his school tasks became increasingly difficult, if not impossible. He played truant, evinced progressive conflict and maladjustment at school, and became neglectful of personal hygiene. His nervousness became aggravated by insomnia, and to relieve his troubled mind he would knock his head against the wall, for as much as a half hour at a time, according to his family (probably a masochistic atonement for guilt arising from his fancied and real sins).

In July, 1928, he was brought to the Children's Court for having taken young girls on three occasions to a sand pile, removing their clothes, and inspecting and manipulating their bodies. He was also reported as possessed of a mania for examining young children's bodies and slapping them on the buttocks, but without any actual attempt to hurt them. The clinic examination revealed a schizoid personality. He admitted that he had, through dishonest means, come into secret possession of a book on "artists and models" several years before, and that through constant gazing at the nude pictures in this and other literature he became so abnormally aroused sexually that he feared for his mind. He made abortive attempts to check his phantasy existence and compulsions, but found himself too weak for the task. His I.Q. was found to be 75, and his mental age 10 years, 9 months. He was in the seventh grade at school. He was remanded to the Children's Psychiatric Division of Bellevue Hospital for observation, study, and treatment, and upon his return to the court was placed on probation.

In 1929 he was arrested for indecent exposure to girls. He received a suspended sentence in a magistrate's court.

In February, 1930, at the age of 17, he was arrested for impairing the morals of a minor, and was committed to the House of Refuge, through the Court of Special Sessions.

In September, 1932, he appeared in the Special Sessions Court of Kings County, for luring a young girl behind a sand pile and stripping off her clothes. He was committed on an indeterminate sentence to Elmira Reformatory. He was paroled in August, 1935, and has since continued to live with his family in the Bronx, without further known detriment to society.

Case C. F. This was a white Protestant boy of 15 years and 11 months at the time of a Children's Court clinic study in August, 1928. He was born in New York City of native parents. His mother had died the year before his appearance in court, and his father had remarried shortly after. The father was a skilled workman, earning $40 a week. The stepmother was good to the boy, and was known to maintain a clean and orderly home, in a residential part of Brooklyn.

Clarence was an only child. His early developmental history was not available. It was known, however, that he was a habitual truant, and poorly behaved at school. It was also learned that he was ungovernable at home, although the parents sought to shield him during the court appearance. He was a dull, excitable boy, given to moods and impulsiveness. He suffered from nightmares and insomnia, and was a chronic nail biter. His progress at school was slow because of a low I.Q. and lack of interest. He left school at 15, and worked occasionally.

In August, 1928, he was brought to the Children's Court for taking a 7-year-old girl into a cellar and attempting forcibly to assault her. The clinic study revealed a markedly unstable personality, and tics and spasms of the face and body. His I.Q. was 77, and his mental age 12 years, 3 months. He was placed on probation by the court, and revisited the clinic on three occasions. Sex hygiene and general guidance were imparted, but the boy's cooperation was at all times vague and detached.

In November, 1929, he was arrested for grand larceny. He appeared in a magistrate's court, in Brooklyn, and the case was dismissed.

In September, 1932, he was reported to have lured girls into cellars, and to have made a sex attempt on a very young girl. He appeared in the Kings County Court, where he pleaded guilty and received a suspended sentence. He was placed on probation.

Last accounts show him to be single, living with his father in Brooklyn, and assisting him at work in a garage. He is of rather sullen type, but is causing no known difficulties for the community.

Case E. M. This boy was white, Catholic, and 13 years and 2 months old at the time of the court clinic study in September, 1932. He was a native New Yorker, of American parents. His mother had died eight years before, and his father had remarried the year after. The stepmother was strict, but kind to the children. The home was comfortable, and located in an uncongested residential section of Brooklyn, N. Y.

Edward was the third of five siblings, and his older sister had a Children's Court record. He was excitable, impulsive, and nervous. He had suffered from enuresis up to the age of 8. He was truant, had deserted his home, and in June, 1931, had been remanded to the Catholic Protectory for three months. His behavior improved upon his return home, except for his truancy. He was in the fifth grade at school, and not a class problem. He attended church with regularity, assisted with the house chores, participated in street games, and showed a strong leaning to movies.

In September, 1932, he was brought to the Children's Court for having committed sodomy assaults on his younger sister on many occasions. The stepmother became extremely hostile toward the boy on discovering what he had done, and no longer wished to have him at home. The clinic diagnosis was neurotic personality. His I.Q. was 84, and his mental age 11 years, 2 months. He was committed to the Catholic Protectory, where he remained until February, 1934. He was reaccepted into the home by the stepmother. The father worked as superintendent. Edward left high school to work on a truck, earning $15 a week.

In February, 1936, three months after his father had deserted the home, Edward was arrested for committing sodomy upon the same younger sister. A lunacy commission declared him mentally sound, and he was sentenced through the Kings County Court to serve five years at Sing Sing Prison, where he is at present.

The case histories provide individual living pictures of these abnormal people, which no amount of tables and diagrams, with their massed data, could possibly supply. Shaw and McKay[2] emphasize the value of the case history in studies of human problems and behavior, as a supplement to the statistical digests.

The case histories reveal a tendency among adult sex violators of the mixed group to return to their particular original juvenile type of offense. Thus, case I.S. resumed his practice of stripping little girls; H.G. returned to his habit of attacking girls on roofs; C.S. continued his sodomy, and A.G. his homosexual practices, into adult life; C.F. retained his old habit of attacking girls in cellars; and E.M. returned to incest with his younger sister, as soon as his father deserted.

The case histories disclose that six of the eight mixed group sex violators came from broken homes—five of the homes broken through death of parents, and one through divorce and later disappearance of the mother. One subject who is making a good adjustment since his sex violation eight years ago came from an intact home. The other case with an intact home, however, did not fare so well, having been committed to Sing Sing for burglary following his sex violation, although he has been at home for the past two years and thus far seems to have kept out of mischief. There is, perhaps, significance in this high ratio of broken homes, when compared to that found in the total mixed group population (p. 24).

The case histories, furthermore, reveal that all of the mixed group sex failures were past puberty at the time of the clinic studies in connection with their original sex offenses. Since one of every four of the mixed group juveniles was below the age of puberty (p. 50), it could be inferred that prepubescent cases are more effectively deterred from later life sexual failure.

[2] *Op. cit.*

The case history studies fail to reveal any distinctive characteristics whereby one could predict sexual failure in later life for members of the mixed group.

Comparison of the mixed group sexual failures with similar instances in the literature is rendered difficult, because other studies make no attempt to segregate the primary from the mixed type, nor is the criterion of failure always clearly defined. In some reports the sexual cases appear grouped among massed data of tables, labeled "successes and failures," with little further clarification. Healy and Bronner[3] mention 4 per cent of sex failures in adult life, without qualification as to whether any or all of these had been involved in sex offenses, general offenses, or both, in their juvenile careers. Again, in a study of 100 underprivileged adult homosexuals, Henry and Gross[4] disclose that only one case among them had a history of juvenile delinquency, but no data is available as to whether this was of sexual or other nature. A report of the Pennsylvania state Parole Commission[5] indicates that, in a check-up of outcomes among 3,000 adult parolees, the men originally committed for sex offenses appear to have done relatively well on probation as compared with other types of offenders, but again it affords no data on the juvenile careers. The Gluecks, in a study of the adult careers of 1,000 male juvenile delinquents of all types, note[6] that there were 22 adult sex offenders among them, only one of whom had a previous juvenile sex offense record, but this juvenile record is not defined with respect to primary or mixed group characteristics.

In another study of the later careers of 1,000 juvenile delinquents, the Gluecks report 4.7 per cent of sexual failures in the first five-year follow-up period; 2 per cent offended against chastity in the second five-year follow-up period; and 2 per

[3] *Delinquents and Criminals*, p. 170.

[4] Henry, G. W., and Gross, A. A., "One Hundred Underprivileged Homosexuals," *Ment. Hyg. 22:* 591, 1938, p. 594.

[5] Parole Commission of the State of Pennsylvania, *Report*, 1927, Part 2, p. 195.

[6] *Op. cit.*, p. 157.

cent of previous sex offenders appeared in the third five-year follow-up period.[7]

Another study by the Gluecks reveals[8] that among crimes for which 510 young adult offenders in Boston were sent to the reformatory, only 0.9 per cent were violations of a sexual nature, and that 77.2 per cent of these 510 youths had juvenile court records. The data in the literature, therefore, though vague, generally support the findings of this study, that *court-treated juvenile sex offenders do not constitute a serious problem to society in later years on the score of sex offenses.*

It is known that one mixed group failure killed himself when apprehended in a sex violation, but the future careers of the remaining seven sexual failures of the mixed group are still unknown and cannot be predicted. Whether any or all of them are destined to become vicious sex criminals and a menace to society, there is no way of foretelling. It is encouraging to note, however, that none of the sexual violations of the mixed group involved violence, or the molestation of young women or mature females. The adult sex offenses were largely of the sneaky type, involving sly inspection of a little girl's body; a secret attempt to obtain sex gratification with a sister or with some other young girl in the neighborhood, through bribery, deception, or intimidation; or perverted affairs with boys or men. Hence, while mixed group juvenile sex offenders, who are general type delinquents, will be shown to constitute a challenge to society, because of their many violent adult general crimes (see next chapter), they apparently do not constitute a threat to the community on the basis of their adult sexual violations.

The most illuminating finding of the study, however, is that court-treated primary group sex offenders, who represent true sex offenders, are not found to commit sexual offenses in later years.

[7] Glueck, S., and Glueck, E. T., *Juvenile Delinquents Grown Up*, pp. 29, 52, 68.

[8] *500 Criminal Careers*, p. 140.

SUMMARY

There are only ten known adult sexual violations among eight members of the mixed group, and none in the primary group. This is significant when compared to the 451 known juvenile sexual offenses committed by the 256 members of the two groups, before their juvenile court and clinic appearance. Furthermore, since the mixed group failures were general delinquents in their juvenile careers, their adult sexual violations cannot be specifically related to their juvenile sex offenses (see p. 3).

Examination of the full-life case histories of the mixed group sexual failures submitted above reveals that there was no sudden release of violent lust upon reaching maturity, but rather that their adult sexual violations were more or less of the same sneaky type and petty quality as in juvenile life. The case histories provide information that cannot be gained from massed data of tables and diagrams. They disclose that all the mixed sex failures were past puberty at the time of their original juvenile sex offenses; that six of the eight sex failures came from broken homes, a slightly greater ratio than in the total mixed group population; and that four of the eight mixed group sex failures committed general crimes before and after the adult sexual violations.

No specific traits could be established for differentiating cases in the mixed group that are destined to become sex offenders in later life from those that are not.

Comparisons between the mixed group sexual failures of this and other studies are rendered difficult because the latter are not segregated as primary and mixed types. Nevertheless, the reports, in general, reflect favorably on adult outcomes among court-treated juvenile sex delinquents.

A most significant finding of the study is that court-treated primary type offenders that represent true juvenile sex cases, as distinguished from the general delinquents of the mixed group, are not found to commit sexual offenses in later years. The explanation for this remarkable finding will appear among the general conclusions of the last chapter.

Chapter X

ADULT GENERAL FAILURES

A LTHOUGH, as originally stated on page 10, the study is
primarily concerned with sexual crimes, any other crimes
committed in adult life by the juvenile sex offenders will nevertheless be counted and evaluated as failures in the outcomes.
The criterion of failure or success, on the score of general or
nonsexual violations, is the same as for sexual violations
(see p. 12).

The adult general failures account for 33 cases of the mixed
group and for 6 of the primary group. In tabulated form they
appear as follows:

	Primary Group 108 Cases	Mixed Group 148 Cases	Total 256 Cases
General failures	6	33	39
Total violations	6	96	102
major	2	82	84
minor	4	14	18

The vast preponderance of major violations in the mixed
group is readily noted, with 82 such instances in this group
as against only 2 in the primary group. However, even these
two failures cannot fairly be charged to the primary group,
since they were so included only through error, during the
initial stage of collecting and classifying the material (see p. 83).
The case histories of these two failures are submitted for
inspection of the early life events. They disclose conditioning
in general delinquency prior to the original sex offense, which
warrants their inclusion in the mixed group, on the basis of the
original definition (see p. 3).

Case G. F. This was a Protestant Negro boy of 13 years, 8
months, at the time of the Children's Court clinic examination in

May, 1930.   He was born in New York City of native parents.   His
father had died ten years before, and his mother remarried shortly
afterward.   She maintained a clean, comfortable home in a good
neighborhood, in addition to working outside and earning $20 a week
as a domestic.   However, she gave the boy little supervision, and he
drifted of his own accord at great distances from home.   He had a
considerable amount of wanderlust, perhaps in part due to early
childhood rickets and restlessness of body.   He sneaked in subways,
hitched on trucks, and mingled with an undesirable group of boys.
He became habituated to truancy and was unadjusted at school.   His
stepfather was unfriendly to the boy and, at times, actually cruel,
particularly when severely under the influence of liquor.   There was
continual conflict between the parents.   Gerald was the older of two
siblings, his younger brother boarding with a friend of the family, a
not uncommon practice among families of this type.   Gerald had
also learned to peculate.

In May, 1930, he was brought to the Children's Court for visiting
the girls' lavatory in a school in the company of a gang of boys, and
writing obscene words across walls, windows, and floor.   This occurred while the boys were playing truant from their own school.   The
clinic study of Gerald showed him to be of normal personality, but a
weak, suggestible type of boy who required an exceptional amount of
close supervision and guidance.   He was in the seventh grade, his
I.Q. was 98, his mental age 13 years, 4 months.   His parents promised to supervise him and the court placed him on probation.   He
revisited the clinic twice while on probation, was provided with sex
hygiene guidance commensurate with his needs, and cooperated
during probation.

In May, 1931, however, he was returned to the Children's Court
by his parents for ungovernableness, truancy, and for associating
with delinquent companions.   He was placed in Brace Memorial
Farm School.

In January, 1934, he was convicted in General Sessions Court of
petit larceny for the theft of a pocketbook and given a suspended
sentence.   He was placed on probation, which lasted until April,
1936, when he was discharged with a good record.   His subsequent
adjustment was satisfactory, and he came to no further difficulties
with the law.

Case D. G. This delinquent was 15 years and 3 months old at the time of his appearance in the Children's Court clinic in January, 1932 He was a white native Catholic boy of Italian parents. The father had been dead five years. The mother confined herself to the duties of the home, which was located in a congested, gang-ridden section of lower Manhattan, New York City. The family was dependent on public subsidies, and caustically critical of society for not providing them with greater home comforts. One older sibling was a psychopath, with an adult court criminal record. The background was distinctly poor.

Dominick was the youngest of four siblings and was an excitable, impulsive, and restless boy who was given no supervision or concern by his family. His church attendance was alleged to be regular, but his school attendance was haphazard, and he was a serious problem there. He associated with a bad group of boys that bore a reputation of molesting and stealing from neighborhood shopkeepers.

In January, 1932, he was brought to the Children's Court for molesting a young woman, forcibly lifting her skirt, and brazenly propositioning her. He was undoubtedly influenced in the act by an uncle, slightly older than himself, who was with him at the time. The diagnosis of the clinic was brain injury, with unstable personality and epilepsy; there was gross evidence of skull fracture, resulting from a previous head injury. The court dismissed him with a warning, and advised medical attention for his physical condition. His subsequent adjustment was continually poor.

In December, 1936, Dominick was arrested for robbery, and was sentenced in the New York County Court to serve an indeterminate term in the penintentiary.

Mention was made on page 83 of the fact that 12 cases of the primary group should not have been so classified because they had committed twenty juvenile offenses, besides sexual violations, at the time of the original clinic study (see Table 13). In addition to the 2 cases cited, therefore, still another, in which the adult offense was disorderly conduct, i.e., dice playing, belongs to this unit of 12 cases that should properly be included with the mixed group. These three failures are, therefore, to appear *classified with the mixed group cases hereafter.* With the corrections indicated, the tabulation of adult general failures should properly be thus:

	Primary Group	Mixed Group	Total
General failures	3	36	39
Total violations	3	99	102
major (felony)	0	84	84
minor (misdemeanor)	3	15	18

CASE HISTORIES

While the summary data on failures and violations provide convincing information with regard to the frequency and severity of nonsexual offenses among the mixed group adults, it is nevertheless felt that much fuller insight may be gained into the morbid character of these abnormal people from a presentation of some illustrative individual case histories.

Case F. V.   This delinquent, 13 years and 6 months old when he appeared at the court clinic in December, 1928, was a white Catholic boy, born in New York City of Italian parents.   The father owned a butcher shop and earned about $45 a week.   The mother confined her duties to the care of the home, which was maintained in a clean and comfortable condition.   The house, owned by the parents, was located in a fair residential part of Brooklyn, N. Y.

Frank was the second of four siblings.   He was of a moody type, impulsive and restless.   At times he assisted his father in the shop and at other times helped his mother with the household work.   He was highly nervous, talked and walked in his sleep, bit his nails, deserted his home on occasions, and at one time was a stowaway on a trip to the British West Indies.   He kept late hours against the wishes of the parents, and showed increasing evidence of breaking away from family control.   He was also a habitual truant and maladjusted at school.   He was continually seeking and associating with undesirable types of companions, despite warnings of his parents. In November, 1927, he was placed in the Catholic Protectory for two weeks by his parents, through private arrangement, in the hope of checking his undesirable habits.   The improvement in conduct was not lasting, and in July, 1928, he was placed in the Hawthorne Protectory of the Jewish Board of Guardians, again through private arrangements, apparently in a desperate move on the part of the parents to utilize every medium of aid in checking the antisocial drive of their son. The parents were untiring in their efforts to rehabilitate the boy.

In December, 1928, Frank was brought to the Children's Court for enticing a 6-year-old girl into a cellar and attempting to assault her. He was also reported to be masturbating excessively. The clinic diagnosis was "markedly unstable adolescent." His I.Q. was found to be 97, his mental age 13 years. He was placed in a boarding home by the court. Shortly thereafter he reappeared in the Children's Court for violation of probation, and was remanded to the New York Catholic Protectory.

In July, 1930, he once again appeared in the Children's Court, this time for stealing an automobile, and was committed to the House of Refuge. He escaped in October, was recaptured in February, 1931, remained at the House of Refuge until discharged to his parents the following year. He worked in his father's store.

In July, 1934, he was arrested for third degree robbery, convicted in the Kings County Court, and sentenced to Elmira Reformatory.

In June, 1937, Frank was once again arrested for robbery with a loaded revolver, was resentenced to Elmira Reformatory for seven years, and is there at present serving time.

Case R. R. This boy was 15 years and 11 months old at the time of his Children's Court clinic examination in April, 1932. He was a white Protestant boy, born in New York City, of native parents. His father was a skilled workman, earning $45 a week. The home was neat and orderly, and located in a good residential section of Manhattan.

Richard was the older of two siblings, and his early developmental history was without significance. With the onset of adolescence, excessive masturbation led to severe emotional disturbances, with excitability, restlessness, and wanderlust. He lost interest in school programs, became habituated to truancy, and turned strongly to phantasy life and movies. Misunderstanding and conflict developed between the boy and his parents. He became more excitable, stubborn, and sullen, and resorted to desertions of home. In January, 1931, he was brought to the Children's Court for ungovernableness and truancy, and placed on probation. He responded poorly, became more rebellious toward his parents and a greater problem at school. At 15, he left school and worked occasionally. He began to associate with a group of vicious characters, and his sex excitement, phantasies, and demands grew. He developed an affair with a 19-year-old girl who had a foul reputation. He had sex relations with her, and deserted his home because of her.

In April, 1932, he was returned to the Children's Court for violation of probation. The diagnosis in the clinic was that of unstable personality. His I.Q. was found to be 101, his mental age 16 years, 1 month. He ranked among the 4 per cent of adults with highest grades in the mechanical tests. He was returned to probation, visited the clinic on two occasions, was working, and appeared to be making a fair adjustment.

In February, 1933, he was arrested for petit larceny. He pleaded guilty in the Bronx County Court and was given a suspended sentence. He was placed on probation.

In January, 1934, he was arrested for disorderly conduct, appeared in the Jersey City Court and was given a suspended sentence.

In June, 1935, he was arrested for burglary, with possession of a gun. He was committed through General Sessions Court to Walkill Prison. He was paroled in October, 1936.

In May, 1937, he was arrested for burglary with the aid of a gun, and assault, and in General Sessions Court was sentenced to fourteen years to Auburn Prison, where he is serving his term at present.

Case H. L. Henry was a Negro Protestant boy, 11 years and 7 months old at the time of his Children's Court clinic study in May, 1929. His family had migrated from the British West Indies five years before. His father was a laborer, earning $25 a week, and his mother confined herself to home duties; the home was situated in a congested but otherwise fair section of Manhattan, New York City. The father was a weak character, and addicted to periodic desertions.

Henry was the oldest of three siblings. There was little check on his spare time activities, and he readily acquired the unruly habits of the street. He allied himself with the interests, ideologies, and practices of a delinquent group of boys, and soon became rebellious and unmanageable at home. His warped attitudes and behavior constituted a problem at school, although he was not a truant. He still continued his connections with church and Sunday school. In September, 1926, he was brought to Children's Court as a neglected child and was committed to the Colored Orphan Asylum. Upon returning to his home he continued to associate with undesirable companions, and became highly excitable, impulsive, and stubborn. He was restless, enuretic, and bit his nails. He walked and talked in his sleep, kept late hours, and was beyond the control of his family. He now became habituated to truancy, and was a severe problem in the classroom, exposing his privates to the young girls, and constituting a general nuisance and menace.

In May, 1929, he was brought to the Children's Court for taking a neighbor's little girl into the hall bathroom and attempting to assault her. She screamed, despite his threats, and he was apprehended. He was also reported to have been badly behaved at home, peculating, and stealing from neighborhood stores. The clinic study revealed a neurotic personality. He was in the fourth grade, his I.Q. was 79, his mental age 9 years and 2 months. He was placed on probation by the court.

In August, 1929, he was again before the Children's Court for stealing from a store, and was committed to the House of Refuge, where he remained until 1933.

In August, 1934, he was arrested for petit larceny, for which he appeared in the district court. He pleaded guilty and received a suspended sentence. He was placed on probation.

In January, 1935, he was arrested for burglary and was committed to the penitentiary through the General Sessions Court.

In January, 1938, he was arrested for disorderly conduct and placed on six months' probation.

In March, 1938, he was arrested for burglary and petit larceny and recommitted by the General Sessions Court to the penitentiary.

In November, 1939, he was again arrested for burglary. He is in the Tombs awaiting sentence, which this time is likely to be for an extended term, in view of his long record.

Case A. C. This subject was a white Catholic boy, born in New York City of Italian parentage. At the time of the court clinic study in September, 1931, he was 15 years and 2 months old. The parents were noncitizens.   The father owned a tinsmith shop and the mother attended to the duties of her home.   The family lived in a comfortable house which they owned.

Andrew was the second of four siblings, undependable, highly unstable, sullen and rebellious.   He was a confirmed truant, and a school problem.   He left school at 15 to assist his father in the store.

In September, 1931, he made a violent assault upon a 30-year-old woman tenant in his father's house, while her husband was at work. He first propositioned the woman and upon being refused, his sex madness turned to maniacal fury, contributed to in part by a sudden onset of guilt and fear of exposure.   He threw the woman forcibly to the floor, and, between her resistance and his sadistic passion, her face and body were badly injured.   Even the cries and pleas of the woman's little daughter did not deter him from his mad impulse. The woman was taken to the hospital, where she remained unconscious for three days.   When Andrew was brought to the Children's Court, he acted in a surly manner.   His mother sought to shield him by claiming that he was a good boy, and projecting all the blame on the victimized woman.   In the clinic his condition was diagnosed as a a manic episode.   His I.Q. was 85, his mental age 12 years and 10 months.   While at the Children's Shelter, pending disposition, he violently assaulted another boy.   He was committed to the Catholic Protectory, where he attempted sodomy on a boy, and was recommitted to the House of Refuge.

After returning to his parents, his work record continued to be poor.   He was highly unstable.   In June, 1933, he appeared at the Cumberland Hospital, Brooklyn, with a severe bullet wound, apparently incurred during an attempt at robbery.

In May, 1935, he was arrested in Pennsylvania, and spent ten days in jail for illegally riding a train and for disorderly conduct.

In March, 1937, he was arrested for felonious assault and was tried in the Kings County Court before a grand jury, but was dismissed for lack of evidence.   Before the case went to trial, he was studied by a lunacy commission and declared sound in mind.   At this time he was married and living with his wife and two children on home relief.

On February 15, 1938, he was arrested for arson and for endangering lives; he pleaded guilty and was sentenced to Sing Sing Prison for five years, where he is confined at present.

Case W. G. This case was that of a Negro Protestant boy, born in the United States. His mother died nine years prior to his appearance in the Children's Court clinic in May, 1932, at which time William was 14 years old. His father remarried three years after the mother's death, was separated two years later, and thereafter maintained a mistress in the home. The father worked as a laborer on occasion, and in part was supported by public subsidy. The mistress kept the house orderly, but the home was generally considered immoral. William had little supervision outside the home and was in steady conflict with the mistress while in the home. His church attendance was regular. He was in the fifth grade, a habitual truant, and a school problem. He was an only child, and bitterly resented the woman's presence in the home, as well as the attentions paid her by his father. He was of a moody, irritable, and sullen type. He kept late hours, associated with undesirable companions, deserted his home on many occasions, and was generally difficult to manage. He practiced masturbation to excess. In 1931, he was before the Children's Court as a wayward and neglected child, and was placed on probation, but his maladjustment continued.

In May, 1932, he impulsively struck his father's mistress a violent blow on the head from behind, with a heavy broomstick. She never regained consciousness and died the following day. In justice to the boy it may be stated that he had not anticipated the tragic effects of his momentary madness. He was examined in the clinic and diagnosed as a case of severe behavior disorder. His I.Q. was 70, his mental age 9 years, 11 months. He was committed to the House of Refuge. He was subsequently transferred to the New York State Training School and paroled in September, 1934.

In April, 1935, he was returned to the state training school as a parole violator and remained there until January, 1936, when he was reparoled. He continued to associate with bad companions and was highly unstable.

In October, 1936, he was arrested for burglary, and in General Sessions Court was committed to the penitentiary for an indeterminate sentence.

Case M. B. Milton was 15 years and 7 months old at the time of the Children's Court clinic study in December, 1929. He was a native white Jewish boy, of Hungarian parents who were citizens.

The father was an unskilled workman, earning $25 a week, and the mother attended to the home, which was located in a crowded slum district of lower Manhattan, New York City.

Milton, the oldest of four siblings, received little supervision, protection, or guidance, and found himself, at an early age, thrown on his own resources under the pressure and onslaught of vicious groups in his milieu. He lacked the vital fortitude to withstand adversity, abuse, and ostracism from games by the very elements that regularly resorted to stealing to gratify expanded tastes for frequent movies, candy, cigarettes, etc. Originally of a timid and insecure type, he soon achieved and enjoyed a state of compensatory aggressiveness derived from greater and greater identification with gang practices. Truancy and misconduct at school became habitual phenomena, and he progressively grew away from family control. Despite a brilliant mind, he was continually failing in his work and classes. He was highly excitable, unstable, restless, and impulsive. His personality and behavior reflected marked disorganization. He idled away his time at gambling, stealing, visiting pool rooms and movies with his gang. His cooperation was nil. He left school in the eighth grade but refused to look for work. He was lazy, disrespectful to his parents, associated with vicious types of companions, had affairs with diseased women, and contracted gonorrhea.

In December, 1929, he was returned to the Children's Court for a violation of probation. He was diagnosed in the clinic as having a marked behavior disorder. His I.Q. was 110, his mental age 17 years, 4 months. He was committed to the Hawthorne School of the Jewish Board of Guardians, where he remained for two years, and thereafter was under the supervision and treatment of this organization.

In December, 1932, he was arrested for illegal possession of a gun. He was tried in the Court of Special Sessions of New York County, and the case was dismissed.

In May, 1933, he was arrested for robbery with a loaded revolver. He had made a practice of holding up gas stations. He was convicted of the offense in the Bronx County Court and sentenced to Clinton Prison for five years. He was paroled in March, 1938.

In June, 1938, he was returned to Clinton Prison for violation of parole. He is serving an indeterminate sentence there at present.

Case R. W. This boy was 11 years and 9 months old when he appeared in the Children's Court clinic in September, 1929. He was a Negro Protestant boy, born in New York City of British West Indian parents who were noncitizens. The father was a skilled workman, earning $35 a week. The mother kept a clean and comfortable home in a congested, gang-ridden neighborhood of Manhattan, New York City.

Roy was the second of five siblings, and had lived with his grandparents in the British West Indies until two years before his court appearance, when he came to live with his parents. The complexity of the new environment and the influences of delinquent companions wrought quick changes in his personality. There was little supervision by the parents, and the boy became an aggressive member of a vicious gang. School lost interest for him and he became habituated to truancy and frequent movies. He was excitable, rebellious, and in marked conflict with his siblings, who sought to check his delinquency. He suffered from enuresis, kept late hours, and deserted his home on several occasions. He was definitely beyond the control of family and school.

In September, 1929, he was brought to the Children's Court for visiting and living in the home of a white adult degenerate (a Cuban). He remained with this man for four days and accepted sodomy, fellatio, and all types of perversions for the money he derived for visits to movies. The adult sent the boy away only because his wife was returning home. The clinic diagnosed Roy's case as one of neurotic personality. He was in the fourth grade at school, his I.Q. was found to be 80, his mental age 9 years and 5 months. He was placed on probation and later, owing to nonconformity, was committed to the House of Refuge for two years. In January, 1933, he was returned to the House of Refuge for violation of probation.

In August, 1936, under the alias of "Lefty," he was arrested for burglary. He appeared in General Sessions Court and received a suspended sentence. He was placed on probation.

In 1936, he was reported for petit larceny through identification from Washington, D. C.

In December, 1936, he was again arrested for burglary and through the General Sessions Court was committed to the New York City Penitentiary.

In March, 1937, he was arrested for burglary and larceny and re-committed through the General Sessions Court to Sing Sing Prison for two years, where he is at the present time.

Case E. P. Edward was a Jewish boy of Russian-born parents; at the time of the Children's Court clinic study he had reached his fifteenth birthday. His father had died five years before and his mother was an inmate of the Kings Park State Hospital, suffering from a mental illness of many years' duration.

Edward was the younger of two children and had been placed, in June, 1924, in the Hebrew Orphan Asylum, through the Children's Court, because of neglect and lewd behavior, consisting of writing obscene notes to girls in class, and employing foul language and masturbation. After two years he was placed with a maternal grand-mother who was much too old to offer the boy proper supervision, guidance, and control. His older sister had appeared before the Children's Court for a sex affair with a married man, but soon after made a good adjustment, obtained work, and earned her own living.

Edward continued to drift steadily downward while living at the home of his grandmother. He associated with evil companions, kept late hours, resorted to frequent truancy, became highly restless and unstable, acquired a severe nail-biting habit, openly defied his guard-ian, and was extremely disrespectful to her. He was vulgar in habits and practiced excessive masturbation.

In March, 1929, he was brought to the Children's Court. Clinic study revealed an extremely unstable personality. His I.Q. was 70, his mental age 10 years, 6 months. He was in the fifth grade at school. He was committed to the Hawthorne School of the Jewish Board of Guardians by the court, and continued under the super-vision and treatment of this organization.

In April, 1934, the Juvenile Aid Bureau was contacted by Edward's sister, who appealed for advice and assistance in the management of her brother. He was 20 years old at the time. His mother was still a patient at the Kings Park State Hospital. The sister was alarmed by reports reaching her that Edward was associating with criminal characters and that he was suspected of implication in a number of burglaries. As soon as the Juvenile Aid Bureau made contact with the boy he left home, and his whereabouts was impossible to trace.

In September, 1934, however, he was arrested for disorderly conduct in threatening a policeman, and appeared in a magistrate's court, New York City.

In November, 1934, he was arrested for burglary and appeared in the Bronx County Court. He pleaded guilty and received a suspended sentency. He was placed on probation.

In October, 1935, he was arrested for burglary. He pleaded guilty in the Bronx County Court and, while awaiting sentence, he vigorously assaulted two prison keepers, wrested the keys from one of them, and escaped from the prison annex. He was later apprehended and indicted for felonious assault and burglary. He was sentenced to serve five years in Sing Sing. He was later transferred to Comstock Prison, and in June, 1939, was ordered held over for one more year at Comstock Prison, where he is now confined.

Case N. W. This boy was 13 years and 6 months old at the time of the court clinic study in November, 1930; he was Jewish, born and reared in New York City. His father was American-born, a semi-skilled workman of good habits and interested in his family. His mother, of Austrian birth, had grown up highly neurotic and unstable; she was a woman of poor potentials, had been reared in an orphanage. Because of inner emotional stresses and the pressure of care of the younger children, Nathan received little supervision. When he came to difficulties, his mother readily shielded him against the father and reality, preventing the boy from achieving a sense of responsibility. He appeared on the surface well-behaved, attended school and synagogue regularly, was in the eighth grade and not a school problem. Beneath the veneer of conformity, however, there was a steady growth of an unhealthy streak in his personality, which was destined to destroy his usefulness to himself and render him a problem to the community. His mind became astutely absorbed in artifices and skills to evade detection and punishment for various sly indiscretions. He peculated and lied. On one occasion he was apprehended and forced to confess that for a lengthy period he had made false alarm calls to firemen and police to report at a vacant house. He had also made many calls to department stores for truck deliveries to this same house. He derived sadistic pleasure from the annoyance he caused, and ego satisfaction from his skill in avoiding apprehension.

The unhealthy trait achieved greater strength when later reinforced by erotic phantasy and guilt because of onanism.

In November, 1930, he was brought to the Children's Court for luring a young girl from Hebrew school, which he attended, to the vacant house mentioned above, and manipulating and exploring her body. The clinic diagnosis was situational reaction to a poor type home environment. His I.Q. was found to be 101, his mental age 13 years, 8 months. He was placed on probation and his course continued erratic. He was later placed in boarding homes under supervision of the Jewish Board of Guardians, but responded poorly, abetted by the unhealthy reactions of his mother.

In December, 1935, he was arrested for stealing at Macy's department store and referred to the Jewish Board of Guardians for supervision and treatment. He was never truthful in his relationships, and failed to cooperate in the guidance program. He was a continual source of trouble to his parents, made threats to extort money from them, gambled, and idled away his time in moving picture houses. He was lazy, indisposed to work, resorted to vague excuses to escape work, and seemed to get money from shady sources. He was suspected of thieving.

In 1936, he enlisted in the CCC, and was discharged in May for serious misconduct, the details of which are unknown.

In June, 1936, he was convicted of grand larceny and received a suspended sentence in the General Sessions Court of Manhattan, New York City. The Jewish Board of Guardians discontinued their interest in him in August, considering the case hopeless.

In January, 1937, he was brought before the district attorney for extorting money from a girl, on the promise of a lucrative job with the WPA, with which organization he was then "importantly" connected. The case was adjusted without his standing trial. The Jewish Board of Guardians reopened the case. His cooperation was poor. He had many affairs with girls, had many frustrations because his shallowness and dishonesty were readily recognized, and annoyed and threatened several girls, necessitating a warning from the Jewish Board of Guardians that court action would be taken against him. He constantly shirked work. The Board of Guardians terminated his case as unsuccessful in 1938. Here is an instance of a warped character, an unstable, troublesome personality, a swindler, an indolent, criminally minded type, destined to create continual difficulty for the community.

In contrast to the many violent adult general offenses committed by members of the mixed group, as revealed in the tabulation on page 110 and in the sample case histories, only three minor adult general violations appear among members of the primary group, and these are itemized below:

Primary Group General Failures	Types of Violation (All Misdemeanors)
1	Disorderly conduct: street fighting
1	disobeying an officer
1	using slug in subway
Total 3	

Consideration of the sentences imposed for the adult general violations will shed further light on the profound differences that separate the two compared types of juvenile sex offenders. The following tabulation should prove instructive:

Type of Sentence	Primary Group	Mixed Group	Total
State prison	0	11	11
City prison	0	25	25
Correctional school	0	14	14
Probation	1	32	33
Fine	1	2	3
Disposition unknown	1	15	16
Total	3	99	102

It is to be noted that mixed group failures were sent to penal and correctional institutions on fifty occasions during adult life, as contrasted with not a single such instance in the primary group.

The many general crimes committed by the mixed group members cannot be attributed to their juvenile sex offenses, since these boys were known to have been strongly conditioned to general offenses in their juvenile careers, on which basis they were originally segregated from the primary group members. Furthermore, since, in contrast, the 108 primary or true juvenile sex offenders committed only three petty general offenses in adult life, there is no basis for any belief that juvenile sex offenses, per se, condition the individual to commission of later life general crimes.   The many felonies of the mixed group are palpably in direct continuity with the many juvenile general offenses characterizing this group.

A boy's status with regard to puberty, at the time of the original court and clinic treatment (see p. 50), seems to bear on the character of the later life outcomes, since only 3 of the 39 adult general failures were below the age of puberty at the above stated time, which is better than the expected ratio.

As originally planned (p. 9), the outcomes among the Negro members of both groups are compared with the white in the following tabulation:

	Negro Failures		White Failures	
	Sexual	General	Sexual	General
Primary Group	0	0	0	3
Mixed Group	0	6	8	30
Total	0	6	8	33
Percentage relations to totals of each race	0.0	23.1	3.4	14.3

The compared data for the two races warrant the inference that there is a tendency to greater failure in terms of sexual offenses among the white population, and of general offenses among the colored population, in the particular sampling under study.   (See Table 22, Appendix, for comparative ratios of white to Negro sex delinquents in the two groups.)

The items of outstanding significance among the adult general failures, as noted in the case histories, are the markedly poor backgrounds, the unstable and psychopathic personalities of these individuals, the almost inevitable criminal careers that follow, the ever increasing severity of the offenses, the frequency of adult court appearances without apparent deterring effect, the great amount of fruitless labor and cost expended by public and private agencies, in addition to the assumption of great hazards by the community—all in the interest of a vicious group of neurotic, psychopathic, and hopelessly maladjusted individuals. This study, however, is primarily concerned with sexual violations, hence cannot enter upon a detailed consideration of the intricate phases of the criminal findings set forth above, for which other studies must be consulted.

SUMMARY

While the primary aim of the study is to determine the significance of juvenile sexual delinquency in relation to sex offenses in later life, nevertheless, according to original intentions, any type of adult criminal behavior was to be reckoned as a failure and analyzed for significance of relation to the early sex offenses. With this understanding, critical treatment was accorded to 84 nonsexual felonies and 15 misdemeanors among 36 failures of the mixed group, and to 3 minor nonsexual violations among 3 failures of the primary group. The high ratio of failure, on the basis of general offenses among members of the mixed group, is found directly related to the unfavorable factors in the backgrounds, the morbid personalities, and behavior traits of these boys, and their strong conditioning to general offenses during juvenile life (see Diagram 9, p. 82).

The severity of the sentences imposed on the adult general failures of the mixed group corresponds to and reflects the violent nature of their offenses, almost half of them having employed guns and other weapons in holdups, burglaries, and assaults. In 11 instances they were committed to the Sing Sing, Auburn, or Comstock state prison, in 25 instances to city prisons, and in 17 instances to vocational schools of the Department of Correction. In contrast, the three general violations among the 108 members of the primary or true sex offender group represented petty disorderly conduct, one subject receiving a suspended sentence, another being fined a few dollars, and the disposition of the third case remaining unknown. It is evident that the juvenile general delinquencies of the mixed group, and not their juvenile sex offenses, are in direct continuity with the many adult general violations found in this group.

Sample case histories of the mixed group general failures are submitted to illustrate the viciousness of their adult antisocial drives, in relation to morbidity of background and early development.

Puberty seems to be a factor in the outcomes, since cases that were past puberty at the time of the juvenile court treatment, appear in greater than the expected ratio among the adult general failures.

Chapter XI

ALL ADULT FAILURES

INDIVIDUAL phases of the adult sexual and general failures and violations, supplemented by case histories, have received consideration in the two preceding chapters. Attention will now be given to a summary digest of all adult failures and violations, before proceeding to an examination of the adult successes in the next chapter.

FAILURES

On the basis of the criterion established on page 12, and restated on page 90, all the adult failures, sexual and general, are presented in Table 16.

TABLE 16.—*Cases with Adult Failure**

Type of Offense	Number of Cases		
	Primary Group 108 Cases	Mixed Group 148 Cases	Total 256 Cases
Sexual	0	8	8
Burglary (with or without gun)	0	12	12
Robbery (with or without gun)	0	7	7
Larceny	0	4	4
Assault	0	2	2
Disorderly conduct	3	5	8
Arson	0	1	1
Forgery	0	1	1
Total of adult failures	3	40	43
Percentage of failure in each group	2.8	27.1	15.2

All cases with adult sex violations are so listed, regardless of any other offenses they may have committed.

* Only the main offense is listed for each case.

The cases with adult failure shown in Table 16 may be tabulated as follows:

Group	Sex Failures		General Failures		Total	
	No.	Percentage	No.	Percentage	No.	Percentage
Primary	0	0.0	3	2.8	3	2.8
Mixed	8*	5.4	36*	25.0	40	27.1
Total	8	3.1	39*	15.2	43	16.8

* Four cases counted both with the sexual and general failures.

Although the adult general offenses committed by mixed group members seem grave, when contrasted with those in the primary group (see p. 121), they nevertheless, when compared with the outcomes of other studies in the literature, appear rather favorable. Thus, the figure of 25 per cent of general failures of the mixed group in the tabulation above appears to advantage when related to Healy and Bronner's finding[1] of 61 per cent of adult failures in a check of the later careers of Chicago juvenile delinquents (employing a similar criterion of failure). Furthermore, among Healy and Bronner's outcomes were 13 instances of homicide, whereas among the outcomes of this study there was not a single known instance of this kind. Favorable comparison may also be made with the outcomes[2] cited by the Gluecks for Boston youthful offenders, studied five years after having completed parole from a reformatory. The Gluecks found 16 instances of homicide and murder in the after-careers, and 72.7 per cent of their cases were failures within the five year postparole period, by a criterion fairly similar to that employed in this study. Compared to the outcomes presented in the literature, therefore, the total of failures in the series of 256 juvenile sex delinquents, covering a period of six to twelve years from the original court clinic study, accounts for only

[1] *Op. cit.*, pp. 28, 33.
[2] *Op. cit.*, pp. 184, 187.

16.8 per cent of the cases. The excellent cooperation[3] in spirit and practice between the justices of the New York City children's courts and the doctors in the court clinics (see Table 14 and Diagram 10), in the completion of programs for the improvement of the boys, may have contributed to the comparatively favorable results noted, although no quantitative determination of this is possible within the limits of the study.

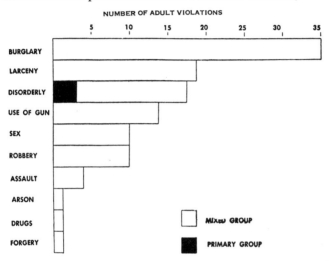

DIAGRAM 11. TYPES OF ADULT VIOLATIONS COMMITTED BY MEMBERS OF TWO
JUVENILE DELINQUENT GROUPS IN LATER CAREERS

VIOLATIONS

The various adult violations represented in Table 17 and Diagram 11 reveal, even more pointedly than the adult failures,

[3] The Gluecks comment on the Boston Juvenile Court and the Judge Baker Foundation Guidance Clinic as follows: "A substantial proportion of the clinic's recommendations were not put into effect by the court (and its agents). . . . But it seems to be a legitimate inference that where so high a proportion of the recommendations of the clinic were not followed by the court, there was something fundamentally weak in the recommendations themselves, or in the practices of the court, or in the relationships of court and clinic to the other agencies": *One Thousand Juvenile Delinquents*, pp. 128, 132.

TABLE 17.—*Total Number of Adult Violations*

Types of Offense	Number of Violations		
	Primary Group 108 Cases	Mixed Group 148 Cases	Total 256 Cases
Sexual	0	10	10
Burglary	0	34	34
Robbery	0	10	10
Larceny	0	19	19
Assault	0	4	4
Use of gun	0	14	14
Disorderly conduct	3	15	18
Arson	0	1	1
Use of drugs	0	1	1
Forgery	0	1	1
Total adult offenses	3	109	112
Percentage of total adult offenses	2.8	97.2	100.0

TABLE 18.—*Types of Sentence Imposed for All Adult Violations*

Type of Sentence	Primary Group 3 Violations	Mixed Group 109 Violations	Total (Both Groups) 112 Violations
	Number	Number	Number
State prison	0	13	13
City prison	0	26	26
Correctional school	0	17	17
Suspended sentence and probation	1 (disorderly conduct)	32	33
Details of disposition unknown	1 (street fight)	18	19
Fine (small)	1 (slugs in subway)	2 (slugs in subway)	3
Total	3	108*	111
Percentage in each group to prison or correctional school	0.0	37.2	

* One adult killed himself when apprehended in a sex violation.

the pronounced differences that separate the two compared types of juvenile sex offenders.

A summary tabulation of all the violations committed by members of the two groups, as they appear in Table 17, should prove helpful.

Type of Violation		Primary	Mixed	Total
		No.	No.	No.
Sexual	Sex attempt with young girl	0	5	5
	Stripping, inspecting young girl	0	1	1
	Self-exposure to young girls	0	1	1
	Sodomy, with younger sister	0	1	1
	with small boys	0	1	1
	Homosexuality with adults	0	1	1
	Total	0	10	10
General	Burglary	0	34	34
	Robbery	0	10	10
	Larceny	0	19	19
	Assault	0	4	4
	Use of gun	0	14	14
	Disorderly conduct, arson, use of drugs, forgery	3	18	21
	Total	3	99*	102
	Total (all violations)	3	109	112

* More than one violation listed per failure.

In the mixed group, the many violent general crimes contrast sharply with the much smaller number of sexual violations of mild type.

SENTENCES

The sentences imposed for the violations are presented in Table 18 and Diagram 12.

A summary tabulation of the sentences imposed by the

criminal courts for the various adult violations, as recorded in Table 18, is presented:

Type of Sentence	Primary Group		Mixed Group		Total Sentences	
	Sex Offenses	General Offenses	Sex Offenses	General Offenses	Sex Offenses	General Offenses
State prison	0	0	2	11	2	11
City prison	0	0	1	25	1	25
Correctional school	0	0	3	14	3	14
Suspended sentence	0	1	0	32	0	33
Fines (small)	0	1	0	2	0	3
Disposition unknown	0	1	3	15	3	16
Total	0	3	9*	99†	9	102

* One mixed group sex offender killed himself.
† More than one sentence listed per adult failure.

The items of suspended sentence and unknown disposition, which have not received comment in previous chapters, will be given consideration here. In addition to the 56 instances of state and city prison and correctional school sentences among mixed group members, there were 50 instances of suspended sentence and unknown disposition.

The 32 cases that received suspended sentence with probation should not be construed to represent harmless events, for not infrequently serious offenses, such as burglary, may bring a suspended sentence, particularly if it is a first adult violation. Thus, case E.P. (p. 119) in 1934 received a suspended sentence for burglary, but the following year he committed burglary and felonious assault on two guards in a jail break, and was sentenced to state prison for five years.   Again, case R.W. (p .117) was placed on probation with suspended sentence for a burglary in 1936, but soon after there followed a rapid series of burglaries, for which he received prison sentences.

The eighteen sentences listed under "disposition unknown" include serious as well as minor offenses. Some of the cases were dismissed, but not necessarily because of the innocence of the offender.   Not infrequently people fear to testify against vicious characters of this type. The sentences of several are still unknown, because of the recency of the arrest, and two

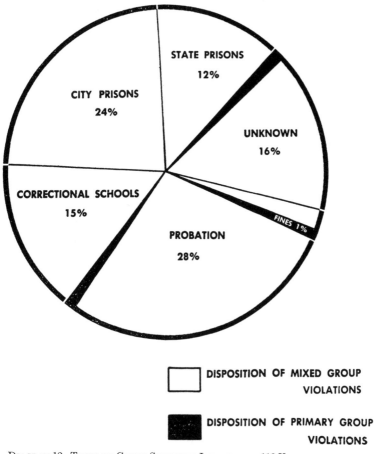

DIAGRAM 12. TYPES OF COURT SENTENCE IMPOSED FOR 112 VIOLATIONS AMONG
JUVENILE DELINQUENTS OF PRIMARY AND OF MIXED GROUP
Mixed group violations include 10 sex offenses

among them are known vicious repeat offenders. In a few cases the details of disposition are not clearly defined. Like suspended sentences, therefore, unknown sentences cannot be construed as insignificant.

The 50 suspended and unknown sentences among the members of the mixed group probably bear as much weight in terms of violence to the community, compared to the 2 instances in the primary group, as the 56 instances of prison and correctional school sentences in the mixed group bear in comparison with the presence of none in the primary group.

SUMMARY

Since the individual phases of adult sexual and general violations have been discussed in previous sections, this chapter confines itself to summary digests.

The adult failures among the compared groups of juvenile sex offenders appear as follows: in the primary group, no adult sexual and 2.8 per cent general failures; in the mixed group, 5.5 per cent sexual and 25 per cent general failures. The critical ratio of the difference between sexual and general failures in the primary group is insignificant, but in the mixed group it is 4.8, indicating high reliability. Total adult failures in both groups equal 16.8 per cent of the series.

The adult violations reveal, even more sharply than the failures, the profound differences distinguishing the two compared groups. Thus, in the primary group are found no sexual and only 3 petty general offenses, whereas in the mixed group are found 10 sexual and 99 general violations, 84 of the latter being felonies, including 34 burglaries, 10 robberies, 19 larceny cases, and 4 serious assaults, many of the crimes being accompanied by the use of dangerous weapons.

Despite the gravity of the adult general offenses committed by members of the mixed group, they nevertheless appear to advantage when compared with other studies in the literature of outcomes among juvenile delinquents. A possible explanation for the comparatively favorable outcomes may be the excellent cooperation between the justices of the children's courts in New York City and the court clinics, in the completion of ameliorating programs for the juvenile delinquents, as shown in chapter VIII (p. 85).

The sentences imposed by the criminal courts give further insight into basic differences between the two compared groups. Thus, 38 per cent of the mixed group failures were sentenced to state or city prisons, or to a state correctional school, as compared with none in the primary group. In addition, there were 50 instances of suspended sentence and unknown disposition in the mixed group, against only 3 such instances in the primary.

Outstanding findings among the outcomes are: the primary or true juvenile sex offender, with the benefit of court and clinic treatment, does not commit sex offenses in adult life and few, if any, petty general offenses; personality and behavior disorders of the mixed group boy, stemming from background factors that are supported by a high critical ratio of difference from the primary group boy, are directly responsible for his many juvenile and adult general offenses, but on the score of sexual offenses he varies only slightly from the primary group boy in early and later life; forecast and treatment for the juvenile sex offender should therefore be based on his background, personality, and general behavior, and not on the nature of his sex offense.

Chapter XII

ADULT SUCCESSES

A S ORIGINALLY stated on page 12, cases with no verifiable record of adult criminal behavior, sexual or other, were to be counted as successes in the outcomes. In accordance with this, juvenile violations following the original clinic study are to be counted among the successes, except in the eleven instances in which the juvenile recidivists became known adult failures.

The successes will thus be treated under the two subheadings:
1. Adult successes with juvenile recidivism.
2. All adult successes (including the continuous successes and those with juvenile recidivism).

1. ADULT SUCCESSES WITH JUVENILE RECIDIVISM

Among a total of 213 adult successes in the two groups, there appear 43 juvenile recidivists who committed a total of 45 juvenile violations following the original study period (Table 19).

The sobering effect of court and clinic contact seems already reflected in the juvenile poststudy period, so that only sixteen sex offenses appear among the two groups, as compared with an original 451. It should prove instructive to compare the original number of sex offenders with the juvenile sex recidivists and with the adult sex failures, in the following tabulation:

Sex Offenders	Primary Group	Mixed Group	Total
Original series (juveniles)	108	148	256
Poststudy (juveniles)	2	13	15
Adult offenders	0	8	8

TABLE 19.—*Juvenile Recidivists and Violations**

Type of Juvenile Violation		Primary Group 108 Cases	Mixed Group 148 Cases	Total 256 Cases
Sexual	Sex attempt with girl	1	3	4
	Sodomy with boys	0	3	3
	Homosexual acts	0	2	2
	Exposure	0	3*	3
	Excessive masturbation	1	1	2
	Heterosexual acts	0	1	1
	Total	2	13	15
General	Stealing	4	10	14
	Burglary	0	2*	2
	Robbery	0	1	1
	Ungovernableness	2	8	10
	Railway violation	0	1	1
	Total	6	22	28
Total		8	35	43
Juvenile violations per 100 cases		7	24	
Percentage of juvenile violations in each group†		22.5	77.5	

* Two violations per case occurred in two instances only.
† Calculated on basis of total violations in two groups per 100 cases.

The data in Table 19 is summarized in the following tabulation:

Type of Juvenile Recidivism	Primary Group	Mixed Group	Both Groups
Sexual	2	13	15
General	6	22	28
Total	8	35	43
Percentage of total recidivists	18.6	81.4	100.0
Percentage of total successes	3.7	16.4	20.1
Percentage ratio of sexual recidivists (to general)	25.0	37.1	34.8

The sex object during the poststudy juvenile period is still in an early stage of evolution, from an object of the same sex to one of opposite sex, resembling more closely the original juvenile offenses (see Table 11, p. 72), than the adult sex offenses (pp. 92, 93). The following tabulation brings this into clearer perspective:

	Violations with Same Sex	*Violations with Opposite Sex*
Original series (juveniles)	252	199
Poststudy (juveniles)	8	8
Adult sex offenders*	2	8

* All are mixed group cases.

No evidence of violence appeared among any of the sex recidivists, and, as among the adult sex failures, the transgressions were largely of the petty, sneaky, or perverted type.

The steady transition toward fewer sexual offenses, with the passage of time, is in sharp contrast to the situation regarding general offenses, as shown in the tabulation below:

Type of Offense		Primary Group 108 Cases No.	Mixed Group 148 Cases No.	Total 256 Cases No.
Sexual	Juvenile (original)	181	270	451
	Poststudy juvenile (recidivist)	2	14	16
	Adult	0	10	10
General	Juvenile (original)	0	287	287
	Juvenile (recidivist)	6	23	29
	Adult	3	99	102

The 43 juvenile recidivists numerically match the total of 43 adult failures, yet the 102 adult general violations, many of them violently criminal in character (see Table 17, p. 128), dwarf in significance the 29 comparatively mild general offenses committed by the juvenile recidivists, with not a single instance of the use of a gun or other dangerous weapon.

Five case histories are presented to illustrate types among the juvenile recidivists. The first 3 cases are all members of the mixed group and represent sexual types of juvenile recidivism, while the last 2 cases, one from each group, represent general types of juvenile recidivism.

Case D. K. This was a Jewish boy, 10 years old when he appeared in the Children's Court in 1928. He was born in New York; his parents were naturalized citizens of Austrian origin. The father was a skilled workman, earning $40 a week. The mother was a poor housekeeper and neglectful of her duties to the children, who were permitted to roam the streets. The home was in a congested part of Brooklyn.

David was of a docile, excitable, and restless type. He associated with undesirable street types and became readily conditioned to their aims and practices. He was the older of two siblings. Defiant of parental control, he became habituated to truancy, and was maladjusted at school. He employed lewd language in the classroom and was a bad influence on other school children.

In May, 1928, he was brought to Children's Court for neglect and because he permitted boys in his neighborhood to commit sodomy on him. Clinic study revealed an unstable personality. His I.Q. was 87, his mental age 7 years. He was placed on probation by the court, and his response was partial.

In March, 1930, he was returned to the Children's Court for ungovernableness at home, truancy and misconduct at school, and for participating in perverted practices. He had been expelled from school for four months, had provoked fights with children, and employed obscene language in the class. He was committed to the Hawthorne School of the Jewish Board of Guardians, where he remained for eighteen months, and thereafter was under the supervision of the Board.

In January, 1936, he was returned to Children's Court for deserting his home, associating with an undesirable group of companions, and being suspected of implication in an arson case. He was committed to the State Training School at Warwick. He found his early adjustment difficult, because of lack of confidence in his own abilities, which

led him into restlessness, impatience, and distrust of others. At
Warwick he was afforded the opportunity to discover that he possessed considerable skill in boxing and in playing a musical instru-
ment, through which he derived great satisfaction, a better mental
outlook toward himself and others, and a lessening of inner anxiety
and tension. He achieved a sense of usefulness, which brought him
confidence and importance. He responded well to routines and trade
training, and in December of the same year was placed on parole to
his parents. He obtained a job, but his adjustment at home was
hampered by misunderstandings with his father, at one time necessitating the establishment of a separate home by David. An improved
situation was achieved through guidance. During the past year, he
has been steadily employed on a truck, earning $16 a week, and living
with his parents in Brooklyn. He and his father have worked out
their conflict, as their quarrels are much less frequent, and it seems
that David is on the way to a satisfactory solution of his chief
problem.

Case A. O.   This boy was 9 years old at the time of his appearance
in Children's Court in June, 1931. He was a white Protestant boy,
born in New York City of native parents. The father had deserted
the family several years before, and the mother lived in common law
relationship with a friend of the family. The mother was a janitress
and paid little attention to her home and family. They lived in a
congested section of the city.

Allen was permitted to drift on his own and became associated
with undesirable companions. He spent his time in moving picture
houses, learned the art of sneaking his way in, lost interest in school,
became a truant and a class problem. He was in the second grade.
He attended church only occasionally. He was the oldest of two
siblings, an unstable, excitable, and enuretic boy. He was a follower
and rather docile.

In June, 1931, he was brought to Children's Court for forcing a
little girl to manipulate his sex organ and also that of his companion.
Clinic study showed him to be neurotic. He was placed on probation,
responded well during probation, and was discharged.

In April, 1933, he again appeared in Children's Court. He was
ungovernable, had peculated at home, and had engaged in sex play

with several boys and girls. He was committed to the Children's Village. He was found to be highly neurotic, and had a difficult time adjusting at the institution. He ran away several times, did not get along well with the boys and staff, and found little interest outside of his music. He played in the band and seemed to enjoy this. He overcame his sex habits and was considered honest.

In August, 1937, after more than four years' residence at the Children's Village, he was discharged to live with his grandparents. He is adjusting well, but continues nervous, introspective, and somewhat seclusive. He has no further record of causing trouble in the community.

Case J. P. The subject was 9 years, 7 months old in December, 1931, when he was studied at the Children's Court clinic. He was a white Protestant boy of native parents. His parents had separated eight years before and the father had disappeared; he had been reported as cruel to the son and heavily addicted to drink. The boy remained with his mother, who had lived with a paramour for five years. She worked out and neglected the boy considerably. The home was situated in a gang-ridden section of Brooklyn.

John, an only child, was excitable, restless, stubborn, and destructive. He was in the third grade, and a problem in school. He was addicted to truancy.

In December, 1931, he was brought to the Children's Court for participating in various perverted practices with an elderly degenerate, as well as with older boys in the neighborhood. He was at the outset induced through pressure, but later began willingly to accept the practices, because of monetary gain. The clinic study revealed a neurotic personality, an I.Q. of 103, and a mental age of 9 years, 11 months. He was placed in various foster homes and his adjustment was poor.

In May, 1937, Mr. P., who had detached himself from his paramours, suddenly reappeared and became reconciled with Mrs. P., who had also freed herself of her friend. The re-established home lasted only two months. The boy continued unruly, kept late hours, and associated with undesirable companions. For a time, he lived with his mother, then with his father. In October, 1937, he was placed by the Gould Foundation in the Y.M.C.A., and worked with his father as an awning man. The father criticized the boy's hours and behavior and John left his father's employment, obtained work as a movie house usher, rented a furnished room and brought girls to it, acquiring a venereal disease. He had to remain several months at the Metropolitan Hospital to be cured of his infection. The father established a better understanding with the boy, and John came to live and work with him.

Clinic recheck in 1938 showed the boy to have profited from his painful venereal condition. He seemed happily adjusted with his father, stating that the latter had succeeded in controlling his drink habit, but that his mother was a disgrace to them and in a deteriorated condition, calling only when needing money for drink; she was morally weak and had a bad reputation.

John seems to have achieved social, sexual, and vocational adaptation and, although the future course is still unknown, there is promise of a satisfactory adjustment, particularly because of his identification and companionship with his father, who himself, after an immoral and stormy career, has improved in character.

Case F. D. This boy was white, Protestant, and 9 years, 2 months old at the time of his appearance in the Children's Court in April, 1929. He was born in New York city of native parents. His parents had separated several months before, the father contributing to the support of the family through the Domestic Relations Court. The parents had been in continual conflict, largely because the father was an irresponsible man, an excessive alcoholic, employed foul language at home in the presence of the children, was cruel, and had a criminal record. The mother worked out, in addition to caring for her own home, which was, however, poorly kept.

Frederick was the youngest of three siblings. He was unadjusted at school, where he was in the 2B grade. He was aggressive, impulsive, and restless. He talked in his sleep and displayed violent temper tantrums.

In April, 1929, he was brought to the Children's Court for wayward conduct at school. It was reported that he would pull suddenly at at girls' bloomers, expose his sex parts to girls in the class, strike other children, and use vulgar language. Clinic study revealed that the boy had sustained a fracture of the skull two years before, and had been in a hospital four weeks, unconscious, vomiting, and suffering headaches. A sharp change in behavior set in subsequent to the head injury. He was diagnosed as a post-traumatic personality. His I.Q. was 98, his mental age 9 years. He was placed on probation, but his response was poor. He made two visits to the clinic, but his conduct was unchanged and his language continued vile.

In February, 1930, he was returned to the Children's Court for truancy and peculations. He was committed to the Children's Village. He responded well to the routines, although mischievous at times, and something of a leader. He remained at the Children's Village until September, 1933, when he was placed at home with his parents under supervision and guidance of the institution. His father drank, and the mother earned the family's living.

The boy continued to make a good adjustment at home, assisting with the house chores and being compliant. The parents separated again, in 1938, because of the father's drinking and indolence. Frederick went to live with his mother and supported her. He worked as an elevator man and has recently purchased a car from his savings. He has apparently made a good adjustment, with the help of a controlled, constructive program of supervision and training, provided during the critical stage of early adolescence.

Case W. W. The subject was 7 years, 5 months old at the time of his Children's Court clinic appearance in November, 1930. He was a Negro Protestant boy who had been reared by a maternal aunt. His father had died six years before, and his mother deserted shortly after, going to the South and leaving the boy with her sister. The mother was never heard from thereafter. The aunt's home was neat and orderly, and located in a fair residential district of Manhattan, New York City. The physical needs of the boy were well provided for, but there was no supervision, because the aunt and her husband worked out all day. The boy fell in with a bad group of boys and even at this early age had already acquired a large store of delinquent skills and vicious behavior.

William was the younger of two siblings, the older one living with another aunt, and there was little contact between the two children. William was aggressive, excitable, stubborn, restless, a bully with other children, talked in his sleep, showed marked tempers, was impulsive and a difficult school problem. He was beyond the control of guardians and teachers. He used foul language at school and began to display serious behavior problems. He exposed himself to little girls, made sex propositions to them, and stole. He kept late hours and peculated at home. Discipline had no effect on him. He was dirty in habits, careless in appearance, and a menace to other children in the neighborhood.

In November, 1930, he was brought to the Children's Court for a sex attempt on an 8-year-old girl in his house. Shortly before that, he suddenly jumped on his 17-year-old cousin, and attempted sex play with her. The guardians suspected that he was masturbating, and they were at a loss to know where he had acquired all his sophistication. Clinic study revealed a markedly excitable and unstable boy. He was in the 1B grade, his I.Q. was 103, his mental age 7 years, 8 months. He was placed on probation, visited the clinic four times, seemed surprisingly well adjusted for the time, and was discharged from probation. His conduct disturbances returned the following year and he was placed in various foster homes. His instability and misbehavior persisted.

In June, 1936, he was brought to the Children's Court for stealing, and was committed to the State Training School for boys at Warwick. He made a fair adjustment at the institution, conforming to school and shop routines, and cooperating with the staff. He was paroled in September, 1937, to live with his aunt and uncle. He was well adjusted in all respects for about a year, when difficulties and misunderstandings arose between the boy and his aunt. William voluntarily returned to the training school in September, 1938, and refused to reconsider returning to his aunt. His emotional stress subsided while at the institution and in March, 1939, he was paroled to live in a Brooklyn foster home, under the supervision of the after-care department of the Warwick institution, and has come into no known further conflicts or difficulties.

Illustrative of the destructive effect of an unusually morbid background on the mind, body, and soul of the child, the following remarkable case history is submitted. The case clearly does not warrant consideration as a success, and yet, on the basis of the original criterion, it cannot fall within the definition of an adult failure, since there is no criminal court record.

Case R. G. This was a Catholic white boy, born in New York City, 9 years, 10 months old at the time of the clinic study in February, 1930. His parents were American citizens of English origin. The mother was syphilitic, melancholic, and had made several suicidal attempts. The father was a semiskilled workman, cruel to his children, and resorted to frequent use of profane language. The home was poorly kept and was located in a slum section of the city. The children received little supervision from the parents.

Robert was the second of five siblings. He was in the second grade at school, a habitual truant, poorly adjusted to class routines. He was generally disorganized in behavior, restless, and sneaky. He was a sly character, busily engaged in the role of business agent for his 11-year-old sister in her various sex ventures. This congenitally syphilitic sister had been under treatment as a sex problem for three years at the Mount Sinai Hospital mental hygiene clinic. In accompanying her on one of her sordid escapades, in which he was preoccupied in picking up extra change as well as in sharing the sister's gains, a group of adolescents, after using his sister, forcibly and brutally performed sodomy on Robert inside an automobile. He may have participated in other such episodes of which nothing was known, but the last event came to the attention of the court authorities.

In February, 1930, the clinic study revealed a psychopathic personality with epilepsy, possibly related to a latent congenital syphilis. His I.Q. was 71, his mental age 7 years, 4 months. He was committed to the Catholic Protectory, where he remained until May, 1931.

In January, 1936, Robert reappeared at the Children's Court for stealing, truancy, and desertion from home. On this occasion he was committed to the Children's Village, where the appearance of major convulsions and mental signs caused his transfer to Rockland State Hospital, where he has remained ever since.

It should be entered upon the record that Robert's younger brother James, 12 years old, is at the present time at the Children's Village for marked behavior disorders—stealing, and on one occasion having caused the death of a passer-by through release of the brakes of a parked car. It is of even greater import to note that Robert's sister, referred to above, is at present an inmate of the Manhattan State Hospital suffering from a mental illness. Agency reports reveal that the parents are totally irresponsible and uncooperative, hardly competent to care for the children, the father now blind from syphilis, while the mother, for reasons already stated, cannot be considered mentally normal.

2. ALL ADULT SUCCESSES (CONTINUOUS SUCCESSES, AND SUCCESSES WITH JUVENILE RECIDIVISM)

The continuous successes account for 170 cases and are differentiated from the 43 juvenile recidivists on the basis of not having been involved in any known type of offense since the original clinic study. The total of 213 adult successes represent 83.2 per cent of the original 256 juvenile sex offenders. The percentage compares favorably with Healy and Bronner's 39 per cent of successes,[1] based on the same criterion as in this study. The critical ratio of the difference is 17.0, showing very high reliability. The later life successes become even more striking when considered with respect to sex offenses only, in which case they total 248, or 96.9 per cent of the original 256 juvenile sex offenders in the two groups, and 108 or 100 per cent in relation to the 108 members of the primary or true juvenile sex offender group.

Whether any of the 213 successes are likely to engage in some type of law violation in future years, is not possible to determine, but the findings cover the span of years when criminal tendencies fully manifest themselves,[2] hence it is safe to assume that the future behavior may be fairly judged by them.

Five sample case histories are presented to illustrate types among the 170 continuous successes. Of the 4 primary group cases, 2 stem from good backgrounds and run a fairly consistent course; one springs from a difficult home setup, is highly dis-

---

[1] *Op. cit.*, pp. 28, 33.
[2] See footnote, p. 1.

organized, but achieves stabilization in an institution; and the last, from a very morbid background, adjusts when shifted to a new and distant environment. The fifth case, belonging to the mixed group, reveals a wretched background and developmental life and a morbid personality, but through a fortunate set of later circumstances achieves a social adjustment. These serve to complete the series of 30 case history reports scattered through the chapters of the section on outcomes.

Case G. C. This was a white Catholic boy, born in New York City of Italian parents, who were citizens. The boy was 10 years, 7 months old at the time he was studied in the Children's Court clinic in September, 1930. His father was a skilled tradesman, earning $40 a week. The mother confined herself conscientiously to the care of the home and children. They were sober, industrious, and constructive people, so that they found it possible on their small income to purchase their own home, which was located in a fair residential section of the Bronx, New York City. George was the youngest of seven siblings, and not one of them had a court record.

George was in the fourth grade, well adjusted at school and regular in his attendance. He visited church and Sunday school regularly, and assisted with the house chores. He received close family supervision and was well behaved.

In September, 1930, he was brought to the Children's Court for a sex offense. It seems that he had observed some older boys "do" things to girls, and through imitation, curiosity, and a desire for "experience," he one day, while playing with a 7-year-old girl in a field adjoining his home, asked her to lie on top of him and placed his organ against her body. He made no attempt and had no intention to employ force or to harm the little girl. Talk among the children in the neighborhood reached the parents of the girl, who became greatly alarmed over the occurrence, and George was brought to court. The clinic study revealed a normal personality. His I.Q. was 83, his mental age 8 years, 10 months. The boy was placed on probation by the court, and revisited the clinic on five occasions, during which general and sex hygiene guidance pertinent to his years were administered. His response to probation was excellent and he was discharged.

He continued to make a good adjustment at home and at school and in his play life. In 1938 the family was still living in the Bronx. Four older children were married and living away from the home. The younger three, inclusive of George, were living with the parents. The father worked as a carpenter, kept close watch over the children, and was very proud of them. The mother was a capable housekeeper and boarded children in her home. George attended high school and worked part time. There were close bonds of loyalty between members of the family and George had a high regard for his parents. He came into no difficulties with the community or law. He continues to be well adjusted, is respectable and sound in morals and ethics. No trace of recidivism has occurred in a period of almost ten years.

Case W. M. This boy was 15 years, 11 months at the time of his clinic study in October, 1930. He was white, Jewish, a native New Yorker, and the son of Hungarian parents. His mother had died ten months before; his father, a semiskilled workman, earned $35 a week and maintained a decent, comfortable home in a residential section of Brooklyn.

William was the third of eight children and was well adjusted at school, where he reached the fifth term in high school. The mother's death worked a profound change in his emotional life. He became moody, sensitive, and introspective. He lost interest in school, which he left several months prior to his court appearance. He began to masturbate excessively and to spend much time daydreaming. He met a Negro pianist who was effeminate and a degenerate. The adult readily victimized the boy, conditioned him to the ideologies and practices of homosexualism. He had the boy sleep in bed with him on nights when his wife was out. He taught William all types of perversions, but the intimacy between the white boy and colored man created suspicion that reached the attention of the Society for Prevention of Cruelty to Children; they investigated and had the boy and the degenerate brought into custody.

In October, 1930, William appeared in Children's Court. The clinic study revealed a normal personality. His I.Q. was 104, his mental age 16 years, 2 months. He was placed on probation when the family promised closer supervision. They were advised to move to a distant neighborhood, which they did. The boy was recently reported as working and living with his family. He has come into no known difficulties with the law since the original episode.

Case J. K. This boy was 13 years, 11 months old in March, 1930, when he appeared in the Children's Court clinic. He was a white Protestant boy, born in New York, of Greek parents who were noncitizens. His father had died ten years before. He was reported as having been a cruel parent, immoral, and a periodic deserter. The mother worked out, in addition to maintaining an orderly home in a fair section of Brooklyn.

John was of a docile type, somewhat nervous, and suffered from enuresis and nail biting. He was the second of four children, a member of the Boy Scouts and of a church club. His church and school attendance was regular. He was well adjusted in school and had reached the eighth grade. When he was 8 years of age, an older boy in the neighborhood had forced sodomy on the boy, and the mother, in confusion and distress, had sought advice on the problem by confiding in an old man who boarded with them. Soon after, this old man, taking advantage of this knowledge, secretly seduced the boy and forced him into the vilest degenerate practices. In order to avoid detection, the man moved from the premises and had the boy visit him in his new quarters, where the perverted practices continued up to the time of the court appearance. The boy was strongly dominated by threats of exposure from the old degenerate, and in addition was tempted by the dollar that he received on each visit. He had become badily demoralized and was forced into committing all types of perversions. As the result of this added nervous strain, John began to stutter.

In October, 1930, the morbid relations with the old degenerate were discovered and John was brought to Children's Court. The clinic study revealed a markedly neurotic personality. His I.Q. was 114, his mental age 14 years, 11 months. He was placed under court supervision in a boarding school, but he continued unstable, and his adjustment was poor. He was thereupon committed to the Children's Village, where he improved in personal cleanliness, worked well, was pleasant, and showed no evidence of continuance of his former sex tendencies. He was returned to his home in August, 1932, but failed to adjust because of the excessive criticism and suspicions of the mother.   John asked to be returned to the Children's Village in November, 1933, which was done, and he remained there until August, 1934, when he was placed with a married sister in Connecticut.   The adolescent instabilities subsided, and he shortly after returned to live with his mother in New York City, where he has been up to the present.   He works steadily and has come to no difficulties with the community or the law.

Case L. N.   This was a white Catholic boy, 12 years, 3 months old at the time of the original Children's Court appearance in May, 1933.   He was born in New York City, his father in England, his mother in Canada.   The parents had separated six years before. The father was an alcohol addict, had a prison record for this, and his whereabouts was unknown.   The mother worked as a janitress and the family was partly maintained by public subsidy.   She had been in prison for larceny in Massachusetts years before.   Beyond bearing the children, she could hardly have been considered a mother, as her attention to the needs and welfare of her children was practically nil.   She had been oppressed by conditions in life, acquired distorted values, and lived a more or less solo existence in the midst of her family.   The home was filthy, in continual disorder, and rife with vulgarity, immorality, and conflict, originally between the parents, and later between the siblings.   This was an ugly family group, and neighbors feared to talk to or about them.

Lawrence was the seventh among eleven siblings, two of whom were in feebleminded institutions, one in an epileptic institution, and two in criminal institutions.   The two criminal older siblings were vicious sex perverts, and the home was slightly better when they were out of it.   The younger children were placed in child care institutions from time to time, but when at home were permitted to roam the streets at will.   The neighborhood was a so-called slum district of lower Manhattan, New York City.   Lawrence was a well-behaved child, despite all these disadvantages.   School and church connections may have operated as balancing factors.   Lawrence attended school regularly and was well adjusted to the routines.   He was, however, of a docile, follower type, tending to seclusion and introspection, rather nervous, and a nail biter.   He was not a happy boy.

In May, 1933, he appeared in the Children's Court as a neglected child and was placed under court supervision.

In September, 1933, Lawrence was brought to the Children's Court for participating in various perversions with the two older criminal siblings, who were back at home. (It should be reported that these two siblings forced or induced two of the younger sisters into sex relations, in consequence of which one of them became pregnant.) It is reported that the mother made no trace of effort to interfere in the morbid happenings in the home, nor was she in the least disturbed over the tragic developments. Clinic study showed the boy to be neurotic in personality; his I.Q. was 80, his mental age 9 years, 9 months. Lawrence was placed with a child care institution for foster home disposition, but shortly thereafter his maternal grandparents took him to live with them in Halifax, Nova Scotia, where he has resided ever since, working and adjusting well. The radical shift in environment was the saving factor in this case.

Case E. H. The boy was 15 years, 3 months at the time of the clinic study in December, 1931. He was a white native Catholic boy, with Austrian parents who were noncitizens. The father had been in a mental hospital for fourteen years, and before that had been reported as immoral, excessively alcoholic, and suffering from syphilis of the brain. The mother had been living with a paramour for thirteen years and this man had died three years before the boy's court appearance. The mother, a skilled worker, earned $40 a week, in addition to attending the chores of her home, which was located in a congested part of the city. A maternal aunt lived in an adjoining apartment and offered the patient such attention as she could spare from her own house duties.

Eugene was the youngest of four siblings; the two oldest were married and out of the home, the third in the Navy. Eugene had been confined to institutions during his entire developmental life, his mother rarely visiting him; neither did anyone else. He grew up with a marked sense of rejection by and hatred toward people. He learned to vent his secret peevishness and hate on defenseless children and animals. He was singularly cruel to the former. He was an aggressive, excitable, envious, impulsive, moody, and sullen boy. He had a tendency to play the bully role among younger children. Shortly before his clinic appearance, he had been taken to his home by his mother, and was supervised by his aunt, but he continued to sense a strange coldness separating him from his mother, his aunt, his cousin, and his siblings.

In December, 1931, he was brought to the Children's Court on the complaint that while alone with his little cousin he wilfully and maliciously burned the little boy's sex organ, and under threat of greater torture had warned him not to reveal anything. Eugene was reported to have derived a morbid delight from the suffering of his helpless victim. It was also stated, although the truth could not be established, that he had propositioned his older married sister for sex relations. The clinic study disclosed a psychopathic type of personality, with an I.Q. of 93, a mental age of 14 years. The boy confidentially admitted that he had in secret practiced sodomy with older and younger boys at the various institutions in which he had been placed. Sex hygiene information was imparted and a better understanding established with regard to his inner impulses and abnormal emotions. He was placed in a childless boarding home, as suggested by the clinic, through the services of the Catholic Home Bureau, where his adjustment proved satisfactory.

In August, 1932, the Catholic Guardian Society was approached for a plan, but it was found that no one among his relatives wished to accept the boy, so that it was necessary to continue him in the boarding home, and he worked part time to help pay his way. Guidance and sympathetic supervision served to tame his impulsiveness and bitterness, and he came into no further difficulties on a sexual or other basis. In 1934, Eugene enlisted in the Marine Corps, and the following year was stationed at the Marine barracks, in South Carolina, where he was adjusting well. It seems that despite an exceptionally morbid early career and an unhealthy personality, he succeeded in rehabilitating himself, as the result of a fortunate change of environment.

SUMMARY

The adult successes total 213, or 83.2 per cent, of the original 256 juvenile sex offenders, including 43 cases with juvenile recidivism and 170 continuous successes. The success percentage compares very favorably with reports in the literature.

Recidivism during the poststudy juvenile period consists of

2 sexual offenses in the primary group, and 14 in the mixed group, and of 6 general offenses in the primary and 23 in the mixed group. Neither the sexual nor the general offenses among the juvenile recidivists are of the violent type. Only two among the recidivists show two offenses, the rest one. Eleven juvenile recidivists are not counted with the successes because of subsequent records of adult failure.

The sobering effect of juvenile court and clinic treatment is reflected not only in the total success percentage, but also in the data of 451 original juvenile sex offenses, 16 poststudy juvenile sex offenses, and 10 adult sex offenses. The adult successes, moreover, become even more striking when considered on the score of adult sex offenses alone, in which case they total 96.9 per cent in the combined groups; rightfully, however, they should be considered 100 per cent, since there are no sexual failures in the primary group, which by original intention (p. 2) was selected to represent true juvenile sex offenders.

Part IV

CONCLUSIONS

THIS STUDY was undertaken to investigate the significance of early sex offenses among males for later life behavior, and in particular to determine to what extent these juveniles become a menace to society, through the commission of sexual or other offenses in adult years. The study also set itself to discover determining factors in the background, personality, and behavior of juvenile sex delinquents, that relate to success or failure in adult life, as criteria in the prediction and treatment of similar cases.

The intensive breakdown of the background, personality, and early behavior traits of the two compared groups, as well as of the later life outcomes with respect to sexual and general offenses, provided rich material for the derivation of the significant findings that appear in the earlier sections of the study. The interpretation of these findings will occupy this part of the study in the following order: conclusions derived from the findings (chap. xiii)—(*a*) answers to original problems (including a statement of limitations), (*b*) unanticipated answers to other problems; general conclusions—prediction, treatment, prevention (chap xiv).

Chapter XIII

DERIVED CONCLUSIONS

N o INCLUSIVE study on the subject of the significance of early sex offenses among males for later life behavior has ever been attempted, to the knowledge of the writer, and no source book exists on the subject. Hence, the exploratory findings contributed by this investigation should prove helpful to workers in the field in their day-to-day dealings with boy sex problems.

The detailed analyses and the large sampling of sex cases make it possible to reach conclusions, in answer not only to the propositions set forth in the statement part of the investigation (pp. 3–5), but also to other problems not considered at the outset. The interpretations and conclusions based on the findings derived from the comparative group analyses of the backgrounds (Part I), personalities, and behavior of the boys (Part II), and their later life outcomes (Part III), are presented in this chapter as follows: (a) answers to original problems (including a statement of limitations); (b) unanticipated answers to other problems.

a) ANSWERS TO ORIGINAL PROBLEMS (INCLUDING STATEMENT OF LIMITATIONS)

1. *What is the relationship of the juvenile to the adult sexual offenses?*

The primary group, representing true juvenile sex offenders, was segregated for specific interpretation and for relation to the adult sexual outcomes (p. 2). In the light of this, the finding of not a single instance of a known sex violation in adult life among the 108 members of the primary group, is of signal importance. This should, nevertheless, not be interpreted to imply that a primary type of juvenile sex offender could never

153

commit a sex offense in later years.   The finding does, however, warrant the conclusion that court- and clinic-treated primary type sex offenders offer excellent prediction possibilities for the future, and that they warrant no concern, anxiety, or suspicion from parents or guardians as to their behavior or outlook.

Even the court- and clinic-treated general delinquents of the mixed group do not perform poorly in later life on the score of sexual violations, only eight failures appearing among the 148 cases.   Furthermore, the ten sexual offenses committed by these failures were of a comparatively mild nature, involving sneak attempts with young girls, or petty perversions with males.   Thus, as against an original total of 451 juvenile sex offenses committed by the 256 members of the two groups, there are but ten adult sex violations in the mixed group, and probably no more, since an adult is not excused from appearing in court for a known sex offense, as in the case of a boy (p. 5).

Court- and clinic-treated juvenile sex offenders do well in later years, on the score of sexual offenses.

2. *Do juvenile sexual offenses lead to later general antisocial behavior?*

From the statistical analyses and the case histories, there is evidence that the adult general offenses stand in direct continuity with the juvenile general offenses, which derive from morbid factors in the background and personality of the individual.   Since such unhealthy factors appear very heavily weighted among mixed group members, it becomes apparent that the juvenile general offenses, common to all of them, and not their juvenile sexual offenses, stand in direct relationship to their later general criminal behavior.   On the other hand, among 108 primary or true juvenile sex offenders there are few morbid factors, many counterbalancing favorable factors, no known juvenile general offenses, and hence but three petty adult general offenses, in contrast to the eighty-four major and fifteen minor general crimes of the mixed group.   From the above, it is patent that juvenile sexual offenses, per se, do not mar the personality of the individual, nor condition him to later general antisocial behavior (pp. 4, 70, 121, 122).

3. *What is the significance of early factors in relation to the outcomes?*

The background, personality, and early behavior traits among the two types of juvenile sex offenders will be interpreted in terms of the favorable and unfavorable outcomes, with the aid of the summary that appears in abridged form in Table 20. Since the study is primarily concerned with *adult outcomes*, instances of juvenile recidivism following the original sex offense, fully evaluated in chapter xii, will not be given consideration here (p. 12).

Careful evaluation of the data serves to disclose that no single factor determines a boy's prospects. Not even the factor of bad neighborhood—than which no other is probably as significant for the personality[1]—of itself fixes the nature of the juvenile behavior, or the later outcomes (p. 41). Again, the unfavorable trait of timidity, found among 31 per cent of the primary group, does not in the least disturb the excellent record of its members in early or later life (p. 62). A single unfavorable factor apparently lends itself readily to mitigation by counterbalancing favorable influences in the home, relatives, school, church, etc., serving to reduce what would otherwise constitute much higher figures of juvenile and adult maladjustment.

A set of early morbid personality factors, common to a large segment of the mixed group population, and almost absent in the primary group, seems to bear strong relationship to the juvenile and adult general offenses of the mixed group. Prominent among these basic factors, derived from the background, are the triad of temperament traits (restlessness, aggressiveness, and stubbornness) and the triad of behavior traits (late hours, gang associations, and demoralizing recreation), with the by-product of school maladjustment (pp. 48, 62).

[1] Shaw *et al.*, *Delinquency Areas*, p. 170.

TABLE 20.—*Salient Background and Personality Factors in Relation to Outcomes*

Factors and Outcomes			No. of Cases		Percentages	
			Mixed Group	Primary Group	Mixed Group 148 Cases	Primary Group 108 Cases
Favorable factors (5)	background	higher education among parents	8	14	5.3	12.9
		better occupation among parents	9	19	6.3	18.1
		home owners among parents	10	17	8.3	18.5
		proper care of home and children	69	91	46.6	84.3
		regular church attendance	56	65	37.6	58.2
Unfavorable factors (15)	background	criminal siblings	19	7	12.8	6.4
		criminal parents	13	5	8.8	4.6
		family dependence on social aid	70	30	47.2	27.7
		bad neighborhood	78	37	52.8	35.1
	personality of delinquent	gang activity	39	2	26.3	1.8
		restlessness (excitability)	109	9	73.6	8.3
		rebelliousness	63	5	42.5	4.6
		habitual late hours	47	0	31.7	0.0
		demoralizing recreation	16	1	10.8	0.9
		school maladjustment	109	5	73.6	4.6
		stubbornness	72	7	48.7	6.4
		nervous disorders	104	35	70.3	32.4
		cruelty	18	1	12.2	0.9
		timidity	20	34	13.5	31.4
		aggressiveness	63	10	42.5	9.2
Later life outcomes	adult violations	sex offenses	10	0	6.8	0.0
		general offenses, major	84	0	56.9	0.0
		minor	15	3	10.2	2.8
	adult failures	sex offenders	8	0	5.4	0.0
		general offenders	36	3	25.0	2.8
	adult court sentences	state prison	13	0	8.8	0.0
		city prison	26	0	17.6	0.0
		correctional school	17	0	11.5	0 0
		probation (social service)	32	1	21.7	0.9
		fines (small)	2	1	1.3	0.9
		disposition unknown	18	1	12.2	0.9

Diagrams 11 (p. 127) and 12 (p. 131) portray glaring differences in the later life outcomes among the two compared groups. Since these cannot stand in relation to the juvenile sexual offenses, which are shown to be fairly similar in the two groups, they obviously relate to factors in the background, personality, and juvenile general behavior, which have been revealed as sharply differentiating the primary from the mixed group. This is supported by a critical ratio of difference ranging from 4 to 8, which denotes high reliability (pp. 32, 39, 47, 69, 87).

To illustrate the operation of different factors of background and juvenile personality in the molding of later behavior, a schematic picture of the evolution of a typical primary and a mixed group boy will be presented. The *primary group boy* develops in a slightly better home and neighborhood; the parents are slightly better educated, and hold slightly better jobs; they are less dependent on public subsidy, and are slightly more constructive; closer supervision and guidance is offered the children; less alcoholism, criminalism, and brutality exist in the parents; slightly higher ethical and moral standards and a greater civic sense prevail in the home; there is a greater family interest and investment in the boy, serving to offset adverse environmental influences. In turn, the boy's response to this is a greater spirit of family loyalty, a greater sense of obligation to conform to home, school, and social requirements, greater self-respect, and a stronger resistance to breakdown of personal and family standards through gang pressure or internal impulses. His personality is more stable, and he exercises greater self-restraint in all behavior, and has a tendency to continue the family tradition of self-improvement, and respect for law and order. A boy with the personality configuration described above, fortified by the confidence and support of his family, could succumb to a new and unprepared-for sex indiscretion and yet quickly rebound to his former poise and become resistant to further sexual or other temptations (Case G. C., p. 145).

The *mixed group boy* compares very unfavorably with the one above described. Fewer good qualities appear among the parents. There are less advantages in the home, less supervision, fewer home ties, more street life, and much stronger conditioning by gang types. In time, the boy is led to ever increasing breaks from family, church, and school controls, serving to bring him into strange relief with accepted standards and requirements. This in turn leads to further disorganization of the personality, as reflected in fear, anxiety, a distrust of society and its institutions, restlessness, rebelliousness, and general nervous tension; there follow desertion of home, maladjustment at school, truancy, late hours, and participation in demoralizing recreational interests. More and more there is a need for and indulgence in all types of predatory and exciting experiences to meet increasing demands for escapes into pleasure, and more and more there is a growing acquisition of skills aimed at the defiance of law and order, and an identification with the ideologies and practices of antisocial elements. There is a progressive abandonment to selfish impulses, and greater participation in juvenile offenses, sexual and other. Juvenile court contacts, clinic guidance, shame, guilt, and family and social exposure have less and less meaning to such personality configuration and less of deterring effect. Among the more strongly fixed of these social psychopaths, self-respect, as well as family and personal identity, are entirely lost. They become dominated only by hate, desire for self-aggrandizement, and a drive for exciting experiences. There is a loss of hope for the future, colored by uncertainty, tension, and impatience to satisfy immediate ends. There is no regard for the law of God or man; further contacts with adult courts and penal institutions serve only to inflame the paranoid and antisocial phases of the personality, with accentuated hostility and viciousness toward the old enemy, organized society, and the onslaught continues more or less unabated, until death (Case H. G., p. 94).

Aside from these descriptions of sharply different personality configurations operating among representative segments of the two groups, variations exist, to the extent that the poorest specimens of the primary group come from worse homes, develop poorer personalities, and behave slightly worse in later life, than the best among the mixed group. Nevertheless, the fact that fundamental differences in background, personality, and general behavior are manifest among mixed group members, as compared with primary, obtains ready confirmation in the finding that the justices of the children's courts committed to juvenile correctional institutions, at the time of the original sex offenses, 39.8 per cent of the mixed group boys, as against only 3.7 per cent of the primary group, despite the fact that on the score of sexual offenses both groups were fairly alike as to severity, frequency, and type of offense (see chap. viii).

The conclusions derived are: that no single factor of background or personality determines a boy's general behavior for good or bad in early or later life; that a set of morbid personality factors, stemming from unhealthy background influences, appear heavily weighted in the mixed group, determining their juvenile general offenses, which are in continuity with the later general crimes; that favorable factors of background and personality account for the absence of juvenile general offenses among primary group members, and for their successful adjustment to social codes in later life (pp. 3, 4, 32, 69, 121).

4. *Do juvenile sex offenders constitute a menace to society in their later sexual behavior?*

Since there are no adult sexual violations in the primary group, which represents true juvenile sex offenders, it is conclusive that court- and clinic-treated juvenile sex offenders are not the source of the vicious sex criminals that prey on society. Even the few adult sexual offenses of the mixed group were sneak attempts with little girls or petty perversions, and did not involve violence to or molestation of young or adult women.

This important item will receive fuller discussion in the final chapter, under general conclusions (p. 106).

5. *Does a specific trait deviant underlie the juvenile and later sexual behavior?*

No specific trait deviant of hereditary, congenital, physical, biologic, or intellectual nature determines the sex offenses in early or later life. Patently, no hereditary or congenital trait deviant could explain the finding that, among 108 primary juvenile sex delinquents, there occurs not a single instance of a known adult sexual violation. Again, no specific physical factor could account for the differences in later life outcomes, particularly since the successful primary group has greater physical handicaps (p. 56). The distribution of the boys on the intelligence scale is from the borderline defective level to the superior, hence surely intelligence could not operate as a specific trait deviant. Lastly, while the analyses reveal that puberty brings an acceleration in the frequency of sex offenses and a greater wilfulness and violence in the sex role, this biologic factor is nevertheless not specific in its effect on the studied cases, since deterring forces tend to check it, as noted in the outcomes. Again, many sex offenses are committed by prepubescents. Furthermore, comparatively few pubescents in the community get into sex difficulties, because of the operation of social, family, cultural, and educational deterrents. Hence, juvenile sex offenses cannot be considered as determined by a specific trait deviant (pp. 50, 53, 81, 92).

6. *How do the sexual and general outcomes compare with those found in other studies?*

Although the general delinquents of the mixed group appear as a vicious aggregation, when contrasted with the primary group on the score of general violations, they nevertheless, when compared with the outcomes among general delinquents in the literature, do not show to disadvantage. The comparison of the mixed group delinquents with general delinquents is warranted, since the former are true general delinquents who in addition engaged in sexual offenses.   As against the 61 per cent of adult failures among Healy and Bronner's juvenile delinquents, on the basis of the same criteria as employed in this study, the 25 per cent of failures in the mixed group shows rather favorably.   Furthermore, while there were many homicides among Healy and Bronner's outcomes, there was not a single known instance of this kind among the outcomes of this study.   Again, the Gluecks' study of outcomes in juvenile delinquents of about the same age range, and on the basis of fairly similar criteria, showed 72 per cent of failures and many homicides (p. 125).

The outcomes also compare favorably, on the score of sexual offenses, with the limited data available in the literature. Thus, Healy and Bronner report 4 per cent of sex failures, which, however, are not segregated as primary and mixed types; this renders proper comparisons difficult, and, furthermore, no information is available in their study as to whether the failures had any records of juvenile sex offenses.   In comparison, nevertheless, with these outcomes, no failures appear in the primary group; and, even if the mixed group failures were included, the total for the series would be 3.1 per cent (p. 104).

The conclusions from the considerations above are: that the general failures of the mixed group compare favorably with outcomes among general delinquents in other studies; that the general failures in the primary group have been shown to be practically negligible; that the sexual failures of the mixed group compare favorably with the meager data in the literature. A comprehensive discussion of the reasons for the more favorable outcomes in this study will appear in the last chapter, but in passing it may be noted that a not insignificant though nonmeasurable factor is involved in the next item.

7. *Did the justices cooperate with the clinics in the completion of programs?*

In dealing with human material with its manifold facets and

complexities of structure and function, it is difficult to relate a behavior result to a specific event of many years back. For this reason, a precise inventory of the beneficial effects growing from the excellent cooperation of the justices and the court clinics in the completion of programs, as revealed in this study, cannot be extracted from the outcomes for specific relationship. Such a purpose could be achieved only through a special study and would probably constitute a task of gigantic magnitude. However, from the comparatively favorable outcomes of the study, a general opinion seems warranted that somewhere in the results there is reflected the remarkable harmony of spirit and practice between the two agencies of the New York City children's courts (see chap. viii).

8. *Do case history reports aid in the understanding of the personalities and outcomes among the compared types of sex offenders?*

Thirty full-life case reports appear in the section devoted to outcomes. They permit clearer insight into the continuity of the background and juvenile personality factors through later life events, than could be achieved through summary data in tables and charts. The significance of the forces in the background and personality of R. G. (p. 143), as they set his life course to terminate in a mental hospital, and that of H. G. (p. 94), ending in a rendezvous with death, would hardly have been gleaned from massed statistical data. The case history is an aid to a fuller understanding of human material, subject to statistical treatment (p. 103).

9. *Do Negro sex offenders fare differently from the white?*

In the comparison of races, the only item of importance appeared in the outcomes, where it was found that adult sexual violations occurred less, and adult general violations more, among the Negro than among the white subjects (p. 122).

10. *Do prepubescents fare differently in later life from post-pubescents?*

All of the sexual and all but three of the general failures of the mixed group were postpubescents at the time of the original sex offense—a finding which suggests that, since the prepubescent cases constitute 25.7 per cent of the total mixed group population, the latter seemingly responded better to deterring influences of the juvenile court and clinic, appearing in far less than the expected ratio among the unfavorable outcomes. It is fair to conclude from this that prepubescent sex offenders respond more effectively to court rehabilitation programs than do postpubescent offenders (pp. 103, 122).

11. *Does the study shed light on the value and soundness of various treatment procedures for boy sex offenders?*

This question will receive full consideration in the next chapter, under the heading of treatment.

12. *Do the findings of the study warrant the transfer of management and treatment of juvenile sex offenders from the courts to the community agencies?*

This question will similarly find answer in the next chapter, under the heading of treatment.

Before proceeding to a consideration of the unanticipated answers, it is proper that a statement be made regarding the limitations to the conclusions.

Limitations. The limitations affecting the conclusions—and there are possibly others than those receiving comment—are of a type to be expected in a large-scale investigation of human material. However, the aim has constantly been to keep the derived values, inferences, and conclusions within the limits of objectivity permitted by the data.

First among the limitations is the fact that the juvenile sex delinquents employed in the study had no fingerprint records to aid in checking their later life careers, in consequence of which some of the adult failures may have been missed. This limitation, however, is obviously unavoidable under present conditions. Moreover, through careful checks and cross checks with the various public agencies, courts, and correctional and penal institutions, as well as criminal identification bureaus, it is reasonable to believe that the number of failures missed has been reduced to a workable minimum.   Again, since the study is concerned with the derivation of values from two compared groups, each containing a large sampling of cases, the effect of possible failure to trace a small percentage (footnote, p. 91) of the cases is likely to be neutralized in the two groups. Lastly, the significant findings derived from the comparative analyses of traits and outcomes (see Parts III and IV and particularly Diagram 11) could hardly have been affected by a change of several cases in one or the other group.   This is supported by the fact that differences in traits and outcomes in the two compared groups are so pronounced that they are sustained by a critical ratio of difference ranging from 4 to 8, which reflects high reliability.

Another limitation is the lack of comparison of traits among the sex delinquents with those in the general population.   In answer, it may be stated that many of the general population data are unreliable because of poor sampling; that comparisons were made where possible; and that the Gluecks[2] emphasize that absence of such comparisons does not vitiate research into the make-up of delinquents.

Another limitation concerns the criterion of success or failure; this receives adequate consideration on pages 10 to 12.   Another limitation is the emphasis placed on failures, rather than successes, in the outcomes.   This is explained by the fact that, in a follow-up of delinquents, the practical concern is whether they become criminals and a menace to society in later years, rather than on the extent to which they are successful in business, happy in life, or live harmoniously with their families (see p. 11).

Still another limitation to be instanced is that feebleminded sex offender cases had been intentionally excluded from the investigation.   However, when consideration is given to the fact that other studies in the literature reveal that the feebleminded, as a group, do not differ materially in personality,

[2] *Op. cit.*, p. 63.

behavior, and outcomes from subjects who are not feeble-minded, the assumption is warranted that no important additional values have been omitted (see footnote, p. 9).

b) UNANTICIPATED ANSWERS TO OTHER PROBLEMS IN MALE JUVENILE SEX DELINQUENCY

In addition to answers to the original problems motivating the research (see pp. 3–5), the intensive breakdown of data for the two compared groups permitted answers to still other problems in the field that had not been anticipated at the outset. These will obtain summary attention.

The investigation made it possible to disprove thoroughly age-worn theories that sexual delinquency is caused by under-age, overage, or disparity in the ages of the parents of the delinquents. The data reveal that only 5 per cent of parents were under 20 years of age, that only 20 per cent were above 40 years, and that the disparity in the ages of the mates at the time of birth of the sex offenders was less than *two* years in over 45 per cent of the cases (p. 16).

An interesting finding of the study is that the court- and clinic-treated mixed group members who commit sexual offenses in later years, do not fulminate into adulthood with violence, as in the case of the general offenses in which half of the mixed group failures employ guns and other dangerous weapons. The conclusion derived from this is that in sex cases the community is afforded ample time and opportunity to protect itself, through proper evaluations of the make-up and prospects of the sexual failures, with a view to either segregation or treatment (p. 105).

A finding of the study, the full significance of which is not yet clear, is that adult sex violators of the mixed group tend to revert to the same type of sex offense as was practiced in juvenile years: thus the delinquent who stripped little girls behind sand piles in early adolescence, commits the same offense in adult life; the one who made sex attempts with girls on the roof, acts similarly in adulthood; the one who took girls into cellars, continues to do the same in later life; the delinquent who performed sodomy on his sister in juvenile life, repeats the act upon the same sister in adult life as soon as his father deserts the home; and so on (p. 103).

The juvenile sex offenders become involved in immoral acts through temptation, curiosity, momentary impulse, bribery, intimidation, a desire for material benefits, a desire to gain the favor of a gang leader, etc.   Most of the boys spontaneously turn away from the sex practices with disgust or fear of exposure, after one or several experiences.   Furthermore, in the entire series of 256 cases, only two boys were found to be so abnormally fascinated by the practices and so affected in personality as to warrant the possible type designation of "homosexual," and only one such actual instance appears among the adult outcomes.   It is, therefore, concluded that juvenile sex offenders should not be referred to or treated as "perverts" or "homosexuals," as is the case, unfortunately, in some of the texts (pp. 87, 93).

Environmental factors, and not hereditary traits, as formerly maintained by Lombrosians and neo-Lombrosians, are shown to be all-important in the general delinquent conditioning of the mixed group members.   However, whereas Shaw and other investigators lay major stress on the neighborhood, this study found it possible, through detailed analyses, to establish that the home rather than the neighborhood is all-significant.   The neighborhood factors operate destructively on a child only when the home standards and controls break down, and the child becomes unprotectedly exposed to the morbid elements of the street (pp. 13, 41, 42).

The study discloses that almost 50 per cent of the delinquents come from homes where one or both parents are dead, or seriously disabled physically or mentally.   This item, when considered in conjunction with other factors, such as poor housing, neglect of home, social dependency, quarreling in the home, deserted, divorced, or separated parents, immoral, alcoholic, and criminal parents, feebleminded and cruel parents, etc., serves to reflect the tremendous amount of social pathology operating in the homes of these boys, with a regular weighting of factors in the mixed group. Cognizance should also be taken of the nonmeasurable factors operating in the homes, such as the favoring of one child against another, unethical attitudes and practices among the parents, rejection of a child by a parent, employment of a child by one parent to spy on the other, influencing of a child's mind by one parent against the other, maltreatment of a nervous or bed-wetting child, etc. Offsetting this ghastly picture to some extent, however, are counterbalancing favorable factors, in one or the other parent, siblings, relatives, school, church, neighbors, etc., without which there would have been far greater juvenile and adult maladjustment among the cases (pp. 31, 47).

The most illuminating and significant finding of the entire study is that, given the benefit of proper court and clinic treatment, juvenile sex delinquency tends to become automatically self-curing. This, however, will be elaborated in the chapter to follow.

Chapter XIV

GENERAL CONCLUSIONS, PREDICTION, TREATMENT, AND PREVENTION

I N ADDITION to the derived conclusions presented in the pre- ceding chapter, there are certain important general con- clusions that only a closely detailed study permits.

GENERAL CONCLUSIONS

A highly significant indication of this investigation is that male juvenile sex delinquency is self-curing, provided the latent forces of shame and guilt, inherent in the moral-cultural pattern, are properly stimulated into action. Under such circumstances a boy's mental faculties are shaken to their very foundation, strong reservoirs of shame are dislodged from attachment to the inactive memories of infantile rectal and bladder control days, and powerful self-generating barriers against recidivism are laid down in the personality, which effectively and lastingly resist a return to sexual offenses. This seems to occur regularly when a sex offense is exposed to a boy's family in the open process of a juvenile court and clinic hearing. No other conclusion seems possible from the outcomes, and the following substantiating findings. Thus, it is common observa- tion for aggressive and calloused juvenile offenders to employ various excuses and defenses in attempts to justify even the most violent general offenses; yet never has a boy appeared in the clinic who sought to *justify* a sexual offense, however insignificant. The same hardened delinquent who is seen to face the consequences of a vicious general assault, or burglary, with complacence, defiance, or indifference, will blush, flounder for answers, and be severely distraught when faced with a charge of even the most trivial sexual offense. The finding of no sexual violations among the 108 members of the primary or true sex offender group tends to support the inference that the latent deterrents of shame and guilt, indoctrinated during the stages of anal, bladder, and onanistic control of infancy and early childhood, are strongly rearoused during the court and clinic exposure of the sex offense, and operate to bring about this remarkable result. Even among the aggressive membership of the mixed group, where the moral-cultural pattern is to some extent nullified by the very low ethical standards and general personality disorganization, only eight sexual failures appear among the original 148 juvenile sex cases, as further support for the conclusion stated. That the aroused forces of shame and guilt may have continued to operate even among the sexual failures, albeit weakly, may be noted from the finding that the few sexual violations were of the sneak and petty perversion type, in contrast to the many violent general crimes committed by the same group of boys. Furthermore, one of the failures, H. G. (p. 94), jumped to his death from a roof top when apprehended in a petty sex offense, evidently because of his inability to face his guilt—for surely, had such a confirmed and psychopathic criminal been faced with the consequences of a robbery or burglary, he would hardly have killed himself; more than likely, his first thought would have been to secure the services of a "good" lawyer.

That sexual offenses are self-curing, because of strong latent forces of shame and guilt inherent in the moral-cultural pattern, and not because of effects instilled or derived from physical contact with the court and clinic, may be noted from the finding that general offenses of the mixed group members, treated by the same court and clinic, showed no such response. On the contrary, in a large segment of the mixed group population, it seems as though general delinquency, instead of operating as a chastening force, tends to condition the offenders to further recidivism. Thus, among the general outcomes of the mixed group, there appear eighty-four major and fifteen minor crimes committed by thirty-six members, for an average of three such offenses per failure; and some of them committed four, five, or six offenses. Hence, it is obvious that, while the juvenile court and clinic labored equally to achieve a cure of the sexual and nonsexual offenders, the ultimate difference in the outcomes rested not with these agencies, but with the existence of powerful inherent deterrents of shame and guilt in relation to sexual offenses, which are woefully absent or impotent in connection with general offenses. Instead of internal shame and guilt, the dominant forces operating in general delinquency are internal hate and external fear, defiance, or anxiety for self-defense.

It is, unfortunately, true that the indoctrinated ethical-cultural pattern is extremely feeble in modern civilization, so that little of guilt or shame arises from the commission of a general offense, and hence insufficient residual or lasting values derive from court exposure of such an offense or from the stimulation employed. This may be exemplified in the attitude and vociferous remarks of an 8-year-old, rather precocious Irish boy, who surely had little leaning toward or grasp of the meaning of communism—but not to the exclusion of seizing upon anything serving his advantage. Thus he said: "Why shouldn't I steal the bicycle? Why should the other kid have a bicycle and me not? He's no better than I am. Why, look at Russia. There everyone is given the same things. What about the bankers, where do you think they get their money? They steal it, that's how they get rich. Look at all of them that's been caught and sent to jail."

These and other expressions permeating the boy's speech served to indicate the extent to which his weak ethical concepts had been nullified and outwitted by his ready defense. There was no trace of internal shame or guilt; instead, his chief concern centered about establishing external personal protection against the outside so-considered unjust world; he felt inwardly secure through a secret consciousness of harboring similar views as his parents, who had already openly condoned the act as a petty affair, common in many children, and occasioned by the influence of other "bad" boys who should be punished, their own being not to blame. This same boy, however, when faced with a petty sex situation on a later day, figuratively melted away. There was not a sign of defiance in his manner or speech. There was no berating the community as unfair, nor any attempt to justify his act. There was total self-condemnation, due to the strong unloosened currents of shame and guilt that shook him to his very core. There was no attempt at display of ego, and no feeling of triumph in glib defensive remarks. He was no longer a martyr or champion of the cause of the "have-nots." He felt exposed and stripped of all protection, even that of his parents, who themselves now were gravely concerned over the disgrace to the family and what the neighbors and relatives might think if they should learn of their son's "depravity." The boy, now distraught within, turned to the outside, not with defiance and justification, but with humility and contrition, seeking help, sympathy, and guidance—a sharply different response from that in relation to his general offense, and hence offering entirely different prospects for prediction and treatment.

The success of the court and clinic contact in checking sexual recidivism, therefore, does not arise from the direct influence of these agencies, but rather from the circumstance that they effectively serve to provoke into action the *internal self-curing processes of shame and guilt*. The precise value of the court in the process rests in its facilities for an impressive exposure of the sex offense to the mind of the boy, with members of the family and strangers about, in the open court procedure, with the addition of the benefits derived from psychiatric reorientation by the clinic. These measures seem to provide the fullest opportunity for arousal of the strong latent currents of shame and guilt, which, with little outside assistance, thereafter can continue to operate within the ego and superego, as a continual fortification of the individual against sexual recidivism.

The study thus successfully brings to light previously un-known basic practical principles that should prove valuable in the treatment of boy sex offender cases by others besides the courts. Any close approximation of the conditions above pos-tulated, on the part of community psychiatric practitioners, agency workers, or even parents, would probably meet with similarly good results, except that parents would have to be particularly well endowed to provide substitute values for the skilled psychiatric approach in sex orientation.

Court- and clinic-treated juvenile sexual offenders are prob-ably not the source of the dangerous sex criminals that disturb society from time to time. From the finding that only eight adult mixed group sex failures, committing sneak acts with little girls or perversions with males, appear among the 256 juvenile sex offenders, comprising all the male sex cases (except the feebleminded) in the New York City court clinics during a period of six years, it does not seem likely that this element is the origin of the vicious sex fiends found in the community. It is probable that adult sex criminals of violent type stem not from court- and clinic-treated cases, but rather from juvenile sex offenders who failed to obtain the benefits of such treat-ment, as in instances where juvenile sex offenders remain unde-tected, where parents hush known sex events through fear of family embarrassment, or where treatment is rendered hap-hazardly and ineffectively. Under such circumstances, with inadequate stimulation of the reactions of shame and guilt, sexual recidivism may, through continued conditioning, become secretly fixed in juvenile life, so that boys of this type may enter adulthood as vicious sex psychopaths, and commit violent crimes of passion, without insight or effective inner deterrents. No such instance appeared among the 256 cases in the series. The inference elaborated above should actually warrant a special study of outcomes among a large sampling of juvenile sexual offenders who have not been treated in court and clinic. However, there is partial support of the view expressed in the interesting item of Henry and Gross,[1] in a recent study of adult homosexuals, showing that only one among a hundred had a juvenile court record, and even this instance is not qualified as to whether this was on the basis of a juvenile general or sexual offense. Another such item appears among the findings of the Gluecks,[2] where, in a survey of the later careers of a thousand juvenile delinquents, twenty-two adult sex offenders are revealed, and only one among them with a previous record of court treatment for a juvenile sex offense; here, however, the particular adult sexual violation is not qualified in regard to whether it was of violent or mild type.

PREDICTION

The later life prospects for the primary type boy are found to be excellent, on the score of sexual or general criminal behavior. No attempt is made, however, to establish whether he is successful in business, happy in his lot, or whether he displays petty conduct deviations in later years; nor is this necessary within the specific confines and aims of this study.

The prediction prospects for the mixed group boy suffer sharply, by comparison with those for the primary group subject, not because of the juvenile or adult sexual offenses, but rather because of unfavorable background, poor personality traits, severe behavior disorders, and the strong conditioning in juvenile and adult general offenses. The investigation reveals that the mixed group behavior disturbances, stemming from background factors, are the forerunners of the juvenile general offenses, which are directly causative of the many and violent adult general offenses. The juvenile behavior disorders of gang association, late hours, demoralizing recreation, and school maladjustment therefore constitute reliable indices for prediction, even in the absence of a record of a juvenile general

[1] *Op. cit.*, p. 594.
[2] *Op. cit.*, p. 157.

offense, on which basis alone the mixed group was originally segregated from the primary.

The prediction prospects for any juvenile sex offender should not be based on the sex offense, but on the criteria of background, personality configuration, nature of response to school and play, and general offensive behavior.

TREATMENT

The findings indicate that juvenile sexual offenders should preferably be brought to court and into the court clinic, in order that they may obtain lasting benefits from maximum stimulation of the inherent self-curing potentialities of shame and guilt, albeit it may involve momentary embarrassment and inconvenience to the family. If the matter is treated privately, there should be no hushing of the sex offense by the family, and every effort should be made to institute effective measures that will arouse an adequate response of guilt and shame in the boy, as a means of laying down permanent deterrents in his mind against recidivism.

Juvenile sexual offenders should be regularly referred to a psychiatrist, if available, for initial study, sex hygiene guidance, and *reorientation of the boy in the presence of his family*. Psychiatric treatment of the juvenile sex offender *should be confined to this original sex orientation*, unless special indications exist, such as enuresis, phobias, inferiorities, general nervousness, mental conflicts, physical maladjustments, school problems, restricted social and athletic life, etc. It is desirable that, after the original psychiatric approach, parents, probation officers, and social workers refrain entirely, unless warranted by circumstances, from any reference to the sex offense in later contacts with the boy, since, as previously indicated, *the condition is self-curing*. Sharp criticism of the juvenile by parents or guardians is uncalled for, and *spying on the boy should be avoided*, lest these operate *adversely* in overfixating the sense of guilt, with possible undesirable sequels of emotional imbalance, inferiority, loss of self-respect, feelings of futility and distrust, and perhaps utter abandon.

While an acquaintance with the psychodynamic principles of psychoanalysis on the part of the psychiatrist is helpful for a proper approach in the process of reorienting the sex delinquent, *orthodox psychoanalytic treatment* of the juvenile sex offender is *not indicated* and *should be avoided*,[3] because of the likelihood of severe and lasting damage to the personality, arising from the long-drawn-out procedure and the inevitable overemphasis on the original sex offense, which is diametrically opposite to the needs of these juvenile cases.

The study reveals that court-treated prepubescents fare much better in later years than postpubescent cases. The obvious implication is that juvenile sex cases should be brought to court and clinic for treatment as early as possible.

Change of neighborhood is often found necessary in sex cases, particularly where knowledge of the immoral events has come into the possession of playmates, schoolmates, or neighbors. Needless to state, change of neighborhood does not imply a move of one or two streets, but a substantial shift to a new environment, to be accompanied, where indicated, by a change of school. It sometimes becomes desirable to place a boy temporarily with relatives until parents can complete their moving arrangements, in which event such relatives should be properly prepared by the court or social worker toward a tolerant understanding of the boy and his needs. Occasionally, a shift of home is mandatory, as when a parent is a poor type of guardian or directly contributes to the boy's original predicament (case L. N., p. 148). Special school adjustments are rarely required in primary type cases, but with mixed group cases, where prob-

[3] Even Sigmund Freud, the "father" of psychoanalysis, in his so-called "bible" of psychoanalysis, the *Collected Papers*, admits the absolute futility of employing psychoanalytic treatment in juvenile life: "I recognize the following limitations in the psychoanalytic method—it demands a certain amount of clear-sightedness and maturity in the patient, and is therefore not suited to youthful persons": *Collected Papers*, vol. 1, p. 245.

lems of curriculum and behavior are common occurrences, changes in program, class, or school may prove helpful in the rehabilitation process, although the school authorities are keenly aware of these requirements and attend to them routinely.

For the general delinquents of the mixed sex group, treatment cannot be concerned with the sex offense alone, since it has been shown that in temperament and general behavior the personalities of these boys are badly warped and that many of them are strongly conditioned to general offenses. Special considerations are therefore necessary for the correction of the general delinquent tendencies among these boys. In mixed group cases arising from broken or disorganized homes, where the boys receive few constructive and many destructive values from family contacts, and where the personalities reveal general rebelliousness, maladjustment, and restlessness at home and at school, with a flare for the unwholesome and antisocial, the boys should be placed in the homes of relatives, in boarding schools, or in institutions, for their own protection as well as that of society.

The institution should be properly equipped to permit a complete revamping of the distorted mental setup of the boy and the elimination of unhealthy attitudes, practices, and interests, through a controlled program of vocational training, education, and guidance directed toward inculcation of regular habits of industry, play, and personal hygiene. There should also be available special facilities for instruction in arts and crafts, music, boxing, and related activities, aiming at re-establishment of a sense of stability and usefulness, of self-respect, and of an appreciation of the rights, feelings, and property of others. Needless to say, if an institution, through necessity, is forced to accept the grave responsibility of salvaging a boy's personality from the evils of a pathologic home, it must aim continually and progressively toward the improvement of standards and means of performance, and be ever on guard against permitting stagnant, disintegrating, or demoralizing influences of spirit or practice to weaken its structure and usefulness.

PREVENTION

The following measures for the prevention of juvenile sex delinquency derive from analyses of the causes (see p. 80) and from studies of the case histories. To counteract the causes, first attention should be directed to sex hygiene guidance of adolescents. This is particularly important because, as shown on pages 50 and 71, pubescents constitute 79 per cent of the juvenile sex offenders in the series, and commit almost all the violent and aggressive sex offenses. Prevention, to be effective, requires that sex hygiene guidance of pubescents be universal. A grave responsibility falls upon the school system, as the only suitable medium through which such guidance may be safely provided for all children past the age of 13, or the approximate age of adolescence.

On this issue Garrison's remarks deserve consideration:

> The proper guidance of high-school pupils by a capable, influential, and conscientious leader can be of great value in developing wholesome attitudes and correct information about various sex problems. The sexual guidance of adolescence is indeed important, from the viewpoint of the welfare and morale of the group; it also demands the greatest care and understanding. One place where sex hygiene teaching can be conducted wholesomely is the school.[4]

Henry indicates the need for careful guidance with respect to sex maladjustments among pubescents by competent psychiatrists, in the following thought:

> Early environmental influences may determine the type of psychosexual pattern, and the pattern of the sex variant is often well established before he reaches adult life.[5]

[4] *Op. cit.*, p. 431.
[5] *Op. cit.*, p. 1025.

Zachry favors school sex guidance in the following words:

> There remains in the minds of some educators, of parents, church-men, and others a question as to the extent to which the school should offer assistance to young people in these aspects of personality development. Some hold that when it comes to sex education the school should withdraw entirely from its educative function in favor of the family or such delegate as it may choose—the private physician or the clergyman. These typical public high-school boys and girls have not received at home as much help as they need in their various perplexities with regard to sex. In numerous instances parents are in fact unprepared—either in emotional adjustment or in possession of factual knowledge—to accept in full the responsibility that some educators would leave wholly to them. Thus this aspect of the adolescent's education, too, is a responsibility of the school, and had best be planned for.[6]

The industrial revolution, which forced the transfer of many former home functions, such as formal education, character building, games and athletics, trade training, and more recently spiritual education, to the jurisdiction of the school, determines that the school shall also undertake sex hygiene education.

Since, under present conditions, the school has not yet accepted this challenge and duty, and since in many homes discussion of any phase of sex is taboo by expressed or suggested standards of the parents, the young adolescent, in the throes of confusion, guilt, and self-condemnation over masturbatory practices, is forced to accept the only educational service available to him—the street. Needless to say, this neither solves his problem nor provides him with security of mind, since through conflicting accounts, misguidance, and disjointed bits of secret and undependable information, which he gains only through precious sacrifice of pride and time, he is left uncertain and alarmed about matters which it is his birthright to know. We adults, through our own stupid system of so-called social

[6] *Op. cit.*, pp. 229–231.

and economic cultural progress, not only rob the adolescent of his natural right to function as a mature male upon reaching puberty, by surrounding him with laws, taboos, fears, guilts, and restrictions that spell for him sexual inhibition until he is old enough to satisfy our conventional concept of marital responsibility (which is usually at an age past 25) but we lack the decency even to provide him with the needed understanding of his sex functions, so that he may at least achieve a reasonable artificial adjustment to his enforced celibacy. In the manner of ostriches, we make no visible recognition of his sex problems, his visceral cravings, not even his simple need of intelligent enlightenment and guidance, by which he might bear his sexual abstinence less stressfully, and view his urge to the substitute sex gratification of masturbation, which comes spontaneously to every boy, in the proper light of control and sublimation, instead of with a plagued mind, guilt, misgivings, misunderstandings, hate, and in terms of stray bits of street information.

The adolescent is therefore not only unfairly deprived, but he is also unjustly condemned for his failure to suppress natural forces beyond his control, while he is denied the only adequate means toward such control via sex hygiene enlightenment. With the many disorganized and broken homes in our community (as well as homes of ignorant and feebleminded parents, homes of ritualistic parents who shy from any mention of sex, homes where parents frankly admit their inadequacy to present the "delicate" subject to their children), it is palpable that suitable sex hygiene education of pubescents on a universal scale is necessary, and could best be achieved by the school system, which alone of all the social agencies has the opportunity of reaching each and every early adolescent at the most crucial period of his life. The schools have at their disposal, or should have, psychiatrically trained personnel to exercise such function. Legal sanction for the program should undoubtedly follow proper publicizing of the issue. Questions as to the precise methods to be employed in sex hygiene guidance of pupils, whether by the individual or the group approach, whether with or without parents' consent, etc., could await later sober reflection and practical determination, with a view toward achieving the best results with the least amount of injury to feelings and prejudices.

Prevention of sex offenses among defenseless, timid, effeminate, and immature children could be achieved through guidance lectures to parents and social workers, as a supplementary service of the school sex hygiene program. General considerations should include the exercise of proper measures of protection of children against the pressure, intrigue, or influence of morbid characters; the procurement of supervised play, boxing instruction, and athletic facilities for them; the provision of a regular spending allowance as an offset to temptation; the selection of well supervised summer camps; and a practical revamping of the present lax legal machinery, with the object of procuring quick and adequate punishment of degenerates who seduce children. Specific items for emphasis should take into view certain basic precepts of prevention. Children should be taught not to accept favors or money from strange men, not to visit strange men's homes, or so-called "clubs," or gang dens, not to idle on corners or in candy store hangouts, not to trust abnormal interest shown them on the part of adults, especially "artistic" and "gifted" types. Special vigilance is to be used by guardians when children obtain toys or money from unknown or uncertain sources. Children should not be left unsupervised in the care of a neighbor's or relative's adolescent boy. Children should not be permitted to sleep together, especially a boy and his adolescent sibling. Parents should not expose their intimate marital sex problems to their children, nor display themselves in scanty dress before them.

It should, however, be realized that the preventive measures listed are hardly expected to filter into homes where parents are psychopathic, feebleminded, criminally minded, or alcoholic, or to be of concern to parents who bring paramours into the home and indulge in debauchery in the presence of their children, parents who abuse children, or parents devoid of morals and character. These and other problems demand the alert attention of the social agencies, if aims and hopes for the building of a healthier younger generation are to become reality.

Regarding preventive measures in relation to the general delinquent of the mixed group, the problem of concern here is not so much the juvenile or adult sex offense, but rather the morbid personality, stemming from unfavorable background factors, which bids strongly for a career of general criminality. Any approach toward the prevention of general delinquency must reach into the home. Very often it is not only the abnormal factors in one parent, but also the meekness or indifference of the other parent who submits to and accepts the demoralizing influences of the mate, that serves to undermine all decent standards and values in the home, and tends to warp the minds of the children so that their approach to life is conceptually distorted, paranoidal, and hostile, rendering them ready victims for further abnormal conditioning by gang and vicious street elements. Such homes make it necessary that society be ever on the alert to step in, albeit uninvited, to protect and, if need be, to remove the children before the damage to personality is beyond repair. Where such neglect abounds, the social agencies that extend into many of these homes, for one or another purpose of assistance, can operate effectively in bringing the condition to the attention of the children's courts, which are vested with authority to protect the health and welfare of the children.

If the home and family life of general delinquents were corrected, neighborhood factors would disappear and with them behavior disturbances from which arise the juvenile general offenses that lead to adult crime. Improvements in the social, moral, and ethical standards as well as in the physical and economic conditions of such homes, are basic to the entire structure of crime prevention, and, though a gigantic undertaking, it nevertheless is a prime challenge to our social order. It is gratifying to note, at this time, that the vast social welfare program undertaken by the present federal administration is striving to achieve the goal of physical and economic security for the underprivileged, and, if well integrated with the efforts of the local welfare agencies most familiar with the intimate needs of these homes, this movement should eventually lead to an improvement in their ethical, cultural, and moral standards as well.

It is hoped that the insights arising from this investigation may prove helpful to social workers, teachers, parents, probation officers, psychiatrists, judges, and institutional personnel in dealing with boy sex problems, and that the study may also serve to stimulate further research in the field. In addition, the intensive analyses of the general delinquents of the mixed group, in comparison with the true sex offenders of the primary group, may contribute to further understanding of the causes of general delinquency and crime, and thereby toward a sound basis for an effectual program of prevention. Finally, boy sex offenses, the prime object of the study, are shown not to constitute a problem to the community, if treated by court and clinic, since the initial hearing and psychiatric reorientation suffice to arouse strong latent moral currents of shame and guilt that operate as effective deterrents against recidivism, the condition thereafter tending to be self-curing.

APPENDIX

FORM 1

Front of coded card

CHILDREN'S COURT DELINQUENCY STUDY

S # C #				Cl Co S Fa
	D	**F**	**M**	
Age				PC Bk PD Pdes PSep PAw
				Con FD MD FDes MDes
Col				SPSep FRm MRm
				UnBk Ilto IlSep
Bp				
Yr				RW P Rel Fos Ins
Cit				ChA Reg Occ None
Rel				UL
H				

OC D: Ir Reg StT HUn HSk HStr I10c Other
     F: Un............St Per Sal............
     DL SSk SeSk SkTr SeP&M P
     M: Un............St Per Sal............
     DL SSk SeSk SkTr SeP&M P HW

ED D: Gr............Ret............IQ............MA............PMA............
     Rea: Int Ill Tro Mov P Con
     Leav: Eco Other   Adj Unadj
     F: El HS Col Inf Ilt   Sp SpR SpRWr
     M: El HS Col Inf Ilt   Sp SpR SpRWr

S   Fu............Ha............St............Li............CtPr............
    OPF 123456789+Y   OPT 123456789+Y

HC Rm............Rn............Per............PerRm............RnPer............
     Brd Ord Dord Imm   Sup: Ex Av None
     ConP ConPS ConS ConPD

BP F: CtPr PDr ExDr FrDr FLan Cru PDes
     M: CtPr PDr ExDr FrDr FLan Cru PDes

NS Cong UnCong Bus Res Gang Play

FORM 1—Continued

Back of coded card

Sa   FamW................ChiW................PhyH................
       BeCl................MenIns................FIns................Epil................

ET   Agg Ca Do Du Exc Jea
       Imp Mo Reb Stu Su

PR   Lead Fol Bully
BT   Enu Sec Smo AttSeek T
ClClass

	Charges	Dates	Act	Disposition
Cur				
Pri				
Sub				

CLR   Ins: ChiCa Cor Prob CtCl HTr
         SchCH Home Recr BB.

ClCont: No................Dur................

Fail: Cl: OnProb AftProb CrCt
       Co: Ins CrCt

REMARKS:

Explanation of coded symbols (some symbols are apparent)

S ⚹ = series no. C ⚹ = clinic no. Cl (etc.) = clinic (source and reliability of data). D = delinquent. F = father. M = mother. Col = color. Bp = birthplace. Yr = yrs. in U. S. Cit = citizen. Rel = religion. H = health. PC = parental continuity. Bk = broken home. PD = parents dead. Con = continuous home. RW = child residing with. P = parents. Rel = relatives. Fos = foster-home. Ins = institution. ChA = church attendance. Reg = regular. Occ = occasional. UL = use of leisure time. OC D = occupation of delinquent. Ir = irregular (etc.). Un = unemployed. St = steady work. DL = day laborer. SeSk = semiskilled. M = managerial. P = professional. SSk = slightly skilled. SeP = semiprofessional. HW = housework. ED D = education of delinquent. Gr = grade. Ret = retarded. PMA = performance mental age. Rea = reason for leaving school. Int = lack of interest. Ill = illness (etc). Adj. = adjusted at school. El = elementary. HS = high school (etc). Si = Siblings. Fu = full. Ha = half. St = step. Li = living. CtPr = court or prison record. HC = home conditions (etc). BP F: = behavior of parents, father. PDr = periodic drunk. NS = Neighborhood setup (etc). Sa = social aid. FamW = family welfare. BeCl = behavior clinic. ET = temperament disorders (etc). PR = play role. BT = behavior traits. T = tantrums. ClClass. = clinic classification. Cur = current violation. Pri = prior. CLR = clinic recommendation. No = number visits to clinic. Dur = duration clinic supervision. Fail = type of failure.

FORM 2

Interview form

Name   Age   Date of birth   Clinic No.   Research No.

Address   P. O.   Family attitude toward interview

Date of original court appearance

Other court appearances

SIGNIFICANT *CHANGES* IN STATUS SINCE COURT APPEARANCE

1. Family continuity

2. Physical health (parents and patient)

3. Mental health of family

4. Financial status (past and present)

5. Home conditions and atmosphere (cleanliness, crowding, order, etc.)

6. Temperance of family and patient (gambling, alcoholism, hours, other vices)

7. Attitude of family and patient toward religion

8. School and vocational progress of patient

9. Patient's present status (special interests, behavior at home, associates, social and sexual interests)

10. Patient's and family's attitude toward one another and toward society

11. Involvements with the law (minor and major law infractions, litigations, traffic violations, court appearances, outcomes, etc.)

12. Interpretation of probable causes for social maladjustments listed under no. 11 above.

(Use other side for additional data)

TABLE 21.—*Ages of Parents at Time of Birth of Delinquents†*

Age of Parent at Birth of Delinquent	Primary Group (108 Cases)				Mixed Group (148 Cases)				Total Cases (256 Cases)			
	Fathers		Mothers		Fathers		Mothers		Fathers		Mothers	
	No.	Percentage	No.	Percentage	No.	Percentage	No.	Percentage	No.	Percentage	No.	Percentage
Under 20 yr.	2	1.8	6	5.5	5	3.5	13	9.0	7	2.8	19	7.4
20–25 yr.	12	11.1	24	22.3	12	8.3	35	23.9	24	9.5	59	23.2
25–30 yr.	19	17.7	17	15.7	26	18.0	32	21.9	45	17.8	49	19.3
30–35 yr.	28	25.9	32	29.7	45	31.3	35	23.9	73	29.0	67	26.3
35–40 yr.	18	16.6	15	13.9	33	22.9	16	11.0	51	20.2	31	12.3
40–45 yr.	20	18.6	12	11.1	13	9.0	14	9.6	33	13.1	26	10.3
45–50 yr.	8	7.4	2	1.8	7	4.9	1	0.7	15	6.0	3	1.2
50–55 yr.	1	0.9	0	0.0	1	0.7	0	0.0	2	0.8	0	0.0
55–60 yr.	0	0.0	0	0.0	2	1.4	0	0.0	2	0.8	0	0.0
Total	108	100.0	108	100.0	144*	100.0	146*	100.0	252*	100.0	254*	100.0

* Ages of four fathers and two mothers unknown.
† Age taken as of last birthday.

TABLE 22.—*Race Distribution of Parents and Delinquents*

Race	Primary Group		Mixed Group		Total	
	No.	Percentage	No.	Percentage	No.	Percentage
White	100	92.6	130	87.8	230	89.8
Negro	8	7.4	18	12.2	26	10.2
Total	108	100.0	148	100.0	256	100.0

TABLE 23.—*Native Countries of Parents and Delinquents*

| Native Country | No. Fathers | | | | No. Mothers | | | | No. Delinquents | | | |
| | Primary Group 108 Cases | | Mixed Group 148 Cases | | Primary Group 108 Cases | | Mixed Group 148 Cases | | Primary Group 108 Cases | | Mixed Group 148 Cases | |
	No.	Per-cent-aeg	No.	Per-cent-age	No.	Per-cent-age	No.	Per-cent-age	No.	Per-cent-age	No.	Per-cent-age
United States	41	37.9	57	38.5	38	35.2	62	41.9	101	93.6	142	95.9
Italy	22	20.5	30	20.3	21	18.4	26	17.6	1	0.9	1	0.7
Russia	8	7.4	20	13.6	7	6.4	15	10.2	1	0.9	0	0.0
Austria	8	7.4	4	2.7	12	11.1	8	5.4	0	0.0	0	0.0
Ireland	5	4.6	7	4.7	5	4.6	8	5.4	0	0.0	0	0.0
Germany	2	1.8	7	4.7	4	3.8	6	4.1	0	0.0	1	0.7
Poland	4	3.8	5	3.4	4	3.8	4	2.7	0	0.0	0	0.0
Greece	5	4.6	2	1.3	3	2.8	2	1.3	0	0.0	0	0.0
British West Indies	0	0.0	5	3.4	0	0.0	5	3.4	0	0.0	1	0.7
All others	13	12.0	11	7.4	14	12.9	12	8.1	5	4.6	3	2.0
Total all nation-alities	108	100.0	148	100.0	108	100.0	148	100.0	108	100.0	148	100.0

TABLE 24.—*Educational Background of Parents of Delinquents*

Type of Education*		Primary Group 108 Cases		Mixed Group 148 Cases		Total 256 Cases	
		No. Parents	Percentage	No. Parents	Percentage	No. Parents	Percentage
Col.	F	4	3.7	2	1.3	6	2.3
	M	1	0.9	1	0.7	2	0.8
H. S.	F	6	5.5	3	2.0	9	3.5
	M	3	2.8	2	1.3	5	2.0
El.	F	79	73.1	106	71.7	185	72.3
	M	81	75.0	111	75.1	192	75.0
Inf.	F	3	2.8	8	5.4	11	4.3
	M	1	0.9	7	4.7	8	3.1
Il.	F	15	13.8	27	18.3	42	16.4
	M	22	20.4	25	16.9	47	18.3
Un.	F	1	0.9	2	1.3	3	1.2
	M			2	1.3	2	0.8
Total	F	108	100.0	148	100.0	256	100.0
	M	108	100.0	148	100.0	256	100.0

* Col. = college. H. S. = high school. El. = Elementary school. Inf. = informal and self-educated. Il. = illiterate. F = father. M = mother. Un = unknown.

TABLE 25.—*Parents' Mastery of English Language Tools*

Type of Tool		Primary Group		Mixed Group		Total	
		No. Parents	Percentage	No. Parents	Percentage	No. Parents	Percentage
Speech	F	104	96.3	137	92.6	241	94.1
	M	101	93.5	128	86.5	229	89.5
Reading	F	83	76.8	108	73.0	191	74.6
	M	79	73.1	110	74.3	189	73.9
Writing	F	83	76.8	105	71.0	185	72.3
	M	79	73.1	108	73.0	187	73.0

F = father. M = mother.

TABLE 26.—*Incomes of Families of Delinquents*

Income Level	Primary Group 108 Cases		Mixed Group 148 Cases		Total 256 Cases	
	No. of Cases	Percentage	No. of Cases	Percentage	No. of Cases	Percentage
High ($15+ per week per family member)	7	9.1	2	1.8	9	4.8
Comfortable ($5–$15 per week per family member)	21	27.3	23	20.7	44	23.4
Poor (Below $5 per week per family member)	49	63.6	86	77.5	135	71.8
Unknown	31		37		68	
Total (all incomes)	108	100.0	148	100.0	256	100.0

TABLE 27.—*Occupational Status of Fathers of Delinquents*

Type of Employment	Primary Sex Cases 108		Mixed Sex Cases 148		Total 256 Cases	
	No. Fathers	Percentage	No. Fathers	Percentage	No. Fathers	Percentage
Managerial	4	3.8	0	0.0	4	1.8
Business	15	14.3	9	6.3	24	10.0
Skilled	23	21.9	42	31.1	65	27.1
Semiskilled (including PWA, CWA, and unskilled)	54	51.5	72	54.1	126	52.5
None	9	8.5	12	8.6	21	8.6
Unknown	3		13		16	
Total (all types of employment)	108	100.0	148	100.0	256	100.0

TABLE 28.—*Housing Conditions and Crowding: Family Rent Status (in Percentages of Groups)*

Rent Status	Primary Group 108 Cases	Mixed Group 148 Cases	Total 256 Cases
	Percentage	Percentage	Percentage
Home owner	18.5	8.3	12.7
High rent ($10+ per person)	21.7	19.4	20.8
Average rent ($5–$10 per person)	36.2	43.7	39.8
Low rent (less than $5 per person)	23.6	28.6	26.7
Total	100.0	100.0	100.0
Crowding*	20.3	27.7	24.6

* Two or more occupants per room.

TABLE 29.—*Social Aid Supplied to Families of Delinquents**

Type of Social Aid	Primary Group 108 Cases		Mixed Group 148 Cases		Total 256 Cases	
	No. Families	Percentage	No. Families	Percentage	No. Families	Percentage
Child welfare only	8	7.4	23	15.5	31	12.5
Family welfare only	10	9.2	11	7.4	21	8.2
Child and family welfare	8	7.4	11	7.4	19	7.4
Physical and mental welfare	1	0.9	10	6.8	11	4.3
All forms of social aid	3	2.8	15	10.1	18	7.0
Total (all social aid)	30	27.7	70	47.2	100	39.1

* In force at time of original study of delinquents in clinics of children's courts. Past social aid to families not considered.

TABLE 30.—*Ordinal Position of Delinquent and Number of Children in His Family (in Percentages of Groups)*

Ordinal Position of Delinquent in Family	1-Child Family		2-Children Family		3-Children Family		4-Children Family		5-Children Family		6-Children Family		7 or more Children in Family		Total	
	P	M	P	M	P	M	P	M	P	M	P	M	P	M	P	M
1st or oldest child	10.2	12.8	10.2	8.8	7.4	4.7	1.8	4.7	0.0	2.0	0.0	1.3	0.0	0.7	29.6	35.7
2d child			7.4	7.4	3.7	6.1	4.6	7.4	3.7	3.4	0.0	2.7	0.9	1.3	20.3	28.8
3d child					6.5	4.1	8.3	4.1	4.6	2.7	0.0	2.0	3.7	3.4	24.1	16.4
4th child							8.3	3.4	3.7	3.4	0.9	0.7	0.9	0.7	13.9	8.2
5th child									2.8	2.0	0.9	2.7	1.8	1.3	5.5	6.2
6th child											0.0	1.3	3.7	0.7	3.7	2.0
7th or beyond													3.7	2.7	3.7	2.7
Total*	10.2	12.8	17.6	16.2	17.6	14.9	23.0	19.6	14.8	12.7	1.8	10.7	14.7	10.8	100.0	100.0

P = primary group. M = mixed group.
* Two families in mixed group not included—number of children unknown.

TABLE 31.—*Frequencies of Status of Delinquents as Only Child, Youngest Child, or Oldest Child*

Status of Delinquent	Primary Group 108 Cases		Mixed Group 148 Cases		Total 256 Cases	
	No. of Cases	Percentage	No. of Cases	Percentage	No. of Cases	Percentage
Only child	11	10.2	19	12.8	30	11.7
Youngest child	42	38.8	50	33.8	92	35.9
Oldest child	32	29.6	52	35.1	84	32.8
Total	85	78.6	121	81.7	206*	80.4*

* With "only child" excluded from the count of youngest and oldest, to eliminate duplication, the following differences would appear in the total figures for both groups: youngest child, 62 (24.2 per cent); oldest child, 54 (21.1 per cent). The grand total of the series would show: only child, 30 (11.7 per cent); youngest child, 62 (24.2 per cent); oldest child, 54 (21.1 per cent); total, 146 (57.0 per cent).

TABLE 32.—*Ratio of Families with Full Siblings to Families with Half-Siblings and Step-Siblings*

Type of Family	Primary Group 108 Cases		Mixed Group 148 Cases		Total 256 Cases	
	No. of Cases	Percentage	No. of Cases	Percentage	No. of Cases	Percentage
With half- and step-siblings	12	11.1	15	10.8	27	10.9
With full siblings	96	88.9	131	89.2	227	89.1
Total	108	100.0	146*	100.0	254*	100.0

* Two families in mixed group, data on siblings (full, half-, or step-) unknown.

TABLE 33.—*Number of Delinquent or Criminal Siblings per Family*

No. of Delinquent Siblings* in Family	Primary Group 108 Cases		Mixed Group 148 Cases		Total 256 Cases	
	No. of Cases	Percentage	No. of Cases	Percentage	No. of Cases	Percentage
1	6	5.5	16	10.8	22	8.6
2	1	0.9	2	1.3	3	1.2
3	0	0	1	0.7	1	0.4
Total	7	6.4	19	12.8	26	10.2

* Besides the offender studied in this survey.

TABLE 34.—*Type of Play among Delinquents*

Type of Play	Primary Group 108 Cases		Mixed Group 148 Cases		Total 256 Cases	
	No. of Cases	Percentage	No. of Cases	Percentage	No. of Cases	Percentage
Supervised and organized	13	12.0	11	7.4	24	9.4
Gang	2	1.8	39	26.3	41	16.0
Unorganized	73*	67.6	85†	57.5	158	62.5
Limited	20	18.6	13	8.8	33	12.9
Total	108	100.0	148	100.0	256	100.0

* Includes 8 cases with type of play life unknown.
† Includes 12 cases with play life unknown, as most appropriately classifiable here, since cases with supervised, gang, and limited play are more regularly and definitely specified in probation officers' records.

TABLE 35.—*Play Role of Delinquents*

Role in Play	Primary Group 108 Cases		Mixed Group 148 Cases		Total 256 Cases	
	No. of Cases	Percentage	No. of Cases	Percentage	No. of Cases	Percentage
Leader	9	8.3	10	6.8	19	7.4
Follower	35	32.4	62	41.9	97	38.0
Bully	11	10.2	48	32.5	59	23.0
Unknown (probably follower)	53	49.1	28	18.9	81	31.6
Total	108	100.0	148	100.0	256	100.0

TABLE 36.—*Church Attendance of Delinquents**

Religious Faith and Type of Church Attendance		Primary Group 108 Cases		Mixed Group 148 Cases		Total 256 Cases	
		No. of Cases	Percentage	No. of Cases	Percentage	No. of Cases	Percentage
Catholic (no Negro Catholics in the series)	regular	37	68.6	39	50.0	76	57.5
	occasional	15	27.7	38	48.7	53	40.2
	none	2	3.7	1	1.3	3	2.3
	total attendance	54	100.0	78	100.0	132	100.0
Protestant (including Negro Protestants)†	regular	14	45.2	15	34.1	29	38.7
	occasional	15	48.4	24	54.5	39	52.0
	none	2	6.4	5	11.4	7	9.3
	total attendance	31	100.0	44	100.0	75	100.0
Jewish (no Negro Jews in the series)	regular	14	60.8	4	15.4	18	36.7
	occasional	9	39.2	18	69.2	27	55.1
	none	0	0.0	4	15.4	4	8.2
	total attendance	23	100.0	26	100.0	49	100.0

* Probation officers' records gave attendance data in all but three records.
† Negro Protestants: regular attendance, 26.2 per cent; occasional, 70.0 per cent; none, 3.8 per cent.

TABLE 37.—*Age Distribution of Delinquents (at Time of Original Court Appearance)*

Age in Years	Primary Group 108 Cases		Mixed Group 148 Cases		Total 256 Cases	
	No. of Cases	Percentage	No. of Cases	Percentage	No. of Cases	Percentage
6	1	0.9	1	0.7	2	0.8
7	2	1.8	0	0.0	2	0.8
8	0	0.0	3	2.0	3	1.2
9	2	1.8	7	4.7	9	3.5
10	7	6.4	11	7.4	18	7.0
11	6	5.5	14	9.6	20	7.8
12	12	11.2	11	7.4	23	9.0
13	21	19.4	22	14.9	43	16.8
14	24	22.4	32	21.6	56	21.8
15	30	27.8	40	27.0	70	27.4
16+	3	2.8	7	4.7	10	3.9
Total	108	100.0	148	100.0	256	100.0

Average (M) age in primary group: 13.7 years.
Average (M) age in mixed group: 13.5 years.
Average (M) age in total of both groups: 13.6 years.

194

TABLE 38.—*Distribution of Delinquents in Pre- and Postpubescent Stages*

Puberty Status	Primary Group 108 Cases		Mixed Group 148 Cases		Total 256 Cases	
	No. of Cases	Percentage	No. of Cases	Percentage	No. of Cases	Percentage
Prepubescent	18	16.6	38	25.7	56	21.9
Postpubescent	90	83.4	110	74.3	200	78.1
Total	108	100.0	148	100.0	256	100.0

TABLE 39.—*Religion of Delinquents*

Group	Catholic		Protestant		Jewish		All Religions	
	No. of Cases	Percentage	No. of Cases	Percentage	No. of Cases	Percentage	No. of Cases	Percentage
Primary	54	50.0	31	28.7	23	21.3	108	100.0
Mixed	78	52.9	44	29.7	26	17.6	148	100.0
Total	132†	51.6†	75*	29.3*	49‡	19.1‡	256	100.0

* Includes whites and Negroes: i.e., whites, 49 (19.1 per cent); Negroes, 26 (10.2 per cent); total 75 (29.3 per cent).

† All whites.

‡ All whites.

NOTE. In the Protestant group, if the Negroes were excluded, the percentage for the total of primary and mixed group cases would be 19.1 (same percentage as for Jewish).

TABLE 40.—*Mental Age and Grade Advancement (in Percentages of Groups)*

Grade Status	Group	6–7 Yr.	8–9 Yr.	10–11 Yr.	12–13 Yr.	14 Yr.	15 Yr.	16+ Yr.	Unknown and Out of School	Total P	Total M
Ungraded	P	0.9	3.6							4.5	
	M	2.0	3.4	2.0	0.7						8.1
1st–4th grade	P	2.7	9.2	1.8						13.7	
	M	5.4	12.2	3.4							21.0
5th grade	P		3.6	6.5	1.8					11.9	
	M		4.7	10.8							15.5
6th grade	P		1.8	5.5						7.3	
	M		1.3	6.8	2.0						10.1
7th grade	P		0.9	7.4	5.6	1.8	0.9	0.9		17.5	
	M			6.8	6.7	1.3		0.7			15.5
8th grade	P			3.7	5.6	1.8	1.8			12.9	
	M			2.0	2.0	3.4		1.3			8.7
High school	P				8.3	0.9	3.7	2.8		15.7	
	M			0.7	2.0	2.7	1.3				6.7
Unknown, out of school	P								16.6	16.6	
	M								14.2		14.2
Total										100.0	100.0

P = primary group. M = mixed group.

BIBLIOGRAPHY

ADLER, A.: *Understanding Human Nature.* New York: Greenberg, 1927.

ALEXANDER, F., and STAUB, H.: *The Criminal, the Judge, and the Public.* New York: Macmillan, 1931.

BLOS, P.: *The Adolescent Personality.* New York: Appleton-Century, 1941.

U. S. Department of Commerce, Bureau of the Census: *Juvenile Delinquents in Public Institutions.* Washington, D.C.: U. S. Dept. of Commerce, 1933.

BURT, C. L.: *The Young Delinquent.* New York: Appleton, 1925.

CARR, L. J.: *Delinquency Control.* New York: Harper, 1941.

Commissioner of Correction, State of New York: *Seventh Annual Report.* Albany, N. Y., 1937.

Domestic Relations Court: *Annual Report,* Legislative Document 85A. New York, 1933.

DOSHAY, L. J.: "Evolution Disproves Heredity in Mental Diseases." *M. J. & Rec., 113:* 148, 1930.

DUREA, M. A.: "Survey of the Extent and Nature of Offenses Committed by Delinquent Boys." *J. Juvenile Research, 19:* 62, 1935.

ELLIS, H. H.: *Studies in the Psychology of Sex,* vol. 6. New York: Random House, 1936.

FREUD, S.: *Collected Papers.* London: Internat. Psychoanalyt. Press, 1924–25, 4 vols.

GARRISON, K. C.: *The Psychology of Adolescence.* New York: Prentice Hall, 1940.

GLUECK, S. S., and GLUECK, E. T.: *500 Criminal Careers.* New York: Knopf, 1930.

———: *Juvenile Delinquents Grown Up.* New York: Commonwealth Fund, 1940.

———: *One Thousand Juvenile Delinquents.* Cambridge, Mass.: Harvard University Press, 1934.

GORING, C. B.: *The English Convict.* London: H. M. Stationery Office, 1913.

GRIMBERG, L. E.: *Emotion and Delinquency.* New York: Brentano, 1928.

GROVES, E. R., and OGBURN, W. F.: *American Marriage and Family Relationships.* New York: Holt, 1928.

HEALY, W.: *The Individual Delinquent.* Boston: Little, Brown, 1917.

———: *Mental Conflicts and Misconduct.* Boston: Little Brown, 1917.

——— et al.: *Reconstructing Behavior in Youth.* New York: Knopf, 1929.

——— and ALEXANDER, F.: *Roots of Crime.* New York: Knopf, 1935.

——— and BRONNER, A. F.: *Delinquents and Criminals.* New York: Macmillan, 1926.

———, ———: *New Light on Juvenile Delinquency.* New Haven: Yale University Press, 1936.

197

HENRY, G. W.: *Sex Variants*. New York: Hoeber, 1941, 2 vols.
—— and GROSS, A. A.: "One Hundred Underprivileged Homosexuals."
   Ment. Hyg., *22:* 591, 1938.
HIRSCH, N. D.: *Dynamic Causes of Juvenile Crime*. Cambridge, Mass.: Sci-
   Art Pub., 1937.
HITSCHMAN, E.: *Freud's Theories of the Neuroses*. New York: Moffat, Yard,
   1917.
KAHN, S.: *Mentality and Homosexuality*. Boston: Meador, 1937.
KEMPF, E. J.: *Psychopathology*. St. Louis: Mosby, 1920.
KIRKENDALL, L. A.: *Sex Adjustments of Young Men*. New York: Harper,
   1940.
KRINSKY, C. M., and MICHAELS, J. J.: "A Survey of One Hundred Sex Offend-
   ers." *J. Crim. Psychopathol.*, *2:* 198, 1940.
LEE, P. R.: "An Experiment in the Evaluation of Social Case Work." *Amer-
   ican Statistics A. J. 23:* 166, 1928 (suppl.).
LOMBROSO, C.: *Crime, Its Causes and Remedies*. Boston: Little, Brown,
   1911.
LUND, D.: *Ueber die Ursachen der Jugendasozialitaet*. Upsala: Almquist and
   Wiksells, 1918.
MACDONALD, A.: *Juvenile Crime and Reformation*. Washington, D. C.:
   U. S. Gov't. Printing Off. 1908.
MOLL, A.: *The Sexual Life of the Child*. New York: Macmillan, 1924.
Parole Commission of the State of Pennsylvania: *Report, Part II*. Philadel-
   phia, 1927.
PAYNE, E. G.: *Principles of Educational Psychology*. New York: New York
   Univ. Press, 1928.
PFISTER, O.: *The Psychoanalytic Method*. New York: Moffat, Yard, 1919.
PLANT, J. S.: "Understanding Sex Delinquency." In Yr. Bk., Nat. Proba-
   tion A., 1932, p. 203.
RECKLESS, W. C., and SMITH, M.: *Juvenile Delinquency*. New York: McGraw-
   Hill, 1932.
ROUSSEAU, J. J.: *Emile*. London: Dent, 1911.
SCHLAPP, M. G., and SMITH, E. H.: *The New Criminology*. New York: Boni
   & Liveright, 1928.
SHAW, C. R., *et al.*: *Delinquency Areas*. Chicago: Univ. Chicago Press, 1929.
—— and McKAY, H. D.: *Social Factors in Juvenile Delinquency*. Report
   on the Causes of Crime, National Commission on Law Observance and
   Enforcement, vol. 2, report 13. Washington, D. C.: U. S. Gov't. Printing
   Off., 1931.
SHIDELER, E. H.: "Family Disintegration and the Delinquent Boy in the
   United States." *J. Crim. Law & Criminol. 8:* 709, 1918.
SLAWSON, J.: *The Delinquent Boy*. Boston: Badger, 1926.
SUTHERLAND, E. H.: *Principles of Criminology*. Philadelphia: Lippincott,
   1934.
TERMAN, L. M., and MERRILL, M. A.: *Measuring Intelligence*. New York:
   Houghton Mifflin, 1937.

THOMAS, W. I., and THOMAS, D. S.: *The Child in America.* New York: Knopf, 1928.

THRASHER, F. M.: *The Gang.* Chicago: Univ. Chicago Press, 1936.

WESTERMARCK, E. A.: *The History of Human Marriage.* London: Macmillan, 1921, 3 vols.

WILE, I. S.: *The Challenge of Childhood.* New York: Seltzer, 1926.

ZACHRY, C. B.: *Emotion and Conduct in Adolescence.* New York: Appleton-Century, 1940.

INDEX

Adolescents, 51, 71, 77

Adult failures, 10, 91. *See also* Outcomes

Adult offenders, *see* Outcomes

Adult sex offenses, *see* Sex offenses

Age: *of* delinquents, 50, 73
  of parents: disparate, 18
    overage, 16, 165
    underage, 17, 165

Alcoholism: *in* parents, 33, 35, 37
  in sex offenders, 65

Ambivalence, 35

Answers: *to* original problems, 153–63
  to unanticipated problems, 165–67

Antisocial behavior, 40, 57, 60, 154, 158

"Artistic" characters, 180

Assault on girls, 76

Attention-seeking, 67

Auto-eroticism, *see* Sex offenses, masturbation

Background factors, 13, 16, 30, 39, 47, 55, 82, 155 ff.

Bad company, *see* Gangs

Bad neighborhoods, 40 f., 155, 166

Basic factors, 3, 48, 62, 70, 155, 156

Behavior disorders, 60, 63
  alcoholism, 65
  attention-seeking, 67
  conflict with family, 67
  delinquency habit, 65
  demoralizing recreation, 44, 155
  destructiveness, 68
  drug addiction, 65
  effeminacy, 66
  enuresis, 65
  gambling, 64
  gang activity, 42, 155, 158
  late hours, 44, 47, 155
  lying, habitual, 68
  movies, 43
  nail-biting, 66

parental, 33 f., 38
  rebelliousness, 67
  relation of: *to* adult outcomes, 48, 70, 155
  to background, 47, 63, 155
  school maladjustment, 44, 48, 155
  sleep disorders, 66
  smoking, 65
  speech disorders, 67
  temper tantrums, 69
  tics, 66

Births resulting from juvenile incest, 77

Broken homes, 24, 32
  in general population, 26
  of Negro deliquents, 24
  of white deliquents, 26

Case histories, 4, 145
  of failures: general, 107 f., 110–21
    sexual, 94–103
  of successes: continuous, 145–50
    with juvenile recidivism, 137–44
  significance of, 103, 162

Causes: *of* criminality, 121, 123, 155 f., 158, 166, 181
  of delinquency: general, 70
    juvenile, 39, 41 f., 48, 70, 158
  of juvenile sex delinquency, 3, 80
    extrinsic, 80
    intrinsic, 81
    specific, absence of, 80, 160

Child sex guidance (male), 177

Children's court clinics: cooperation with justices, 84
  original study in, 1
  recommendations of, 85
  revisits to, 86
  treatment by, 86, 151, 163, 174

Church attendance: *of* general population, 46
  of sex offenders, 46, 156